PRAISE FOR *A BRIEF HISTORY OF FASCIST LIES*

"Federico Finchelstein delivers a vital compendium on a dark seam running through our modern politics. This is not just a deft intellectual history of fascism, but an urgent reminder of the deep well of hate that lies beneath our era of 'alternative facts' and 'fake news.'"

—ISHAAN THAROOR, *Washington Post*

"Finchelstein brings clarity and precision to the debate about the populist far right at a time when pundits across the globe casually throw around the term 'fascist' with little regard for its history or meaning. Ranging from Europe to the United States to Latin America, Finchelstein shows that dismissing contemporary xenophobic populists as insane swindlers does little to weaken or defeat them and merely allows them to keep winning by waging war on the truth."

—SASHA POLAKOW-SURANSKY, author of *Go Back to Where You Came From: The Backlash against Immigration and the Fate of Western Democracy*

"At a time when politicians like Donald Trump and Jair Bolsonaro claim that information they don't like is 'fake news,' Finchelstein's history of fascist lying strikes a chord. From Mussolini onward, truth is what the leader needs it to be."

—RUTH BEN-GHIAT, *Professor of Italian and History, New York University*

"This excellent and timely book does exactly what its title promises. Finchelstein builds upon his well-established record of scholarship on fascism, populism, and authoritarianism, providing a modern history of political lies. He provides concrete historical answers to paradoxical understandings of lies, including one of the most perplexing: why fascists thought that lying serves the truth."

—BENJAMIN C. BROWER, *Associate Professor of History at The University of Texas at Austin*

"In this concise book, the author offers an outstanding analysis on lying in politics, a theme very timely with 'fake news' at the center of our debate on political communication. Here Finchelstein presents an original history of fascist ideology and the context of its diffusion that goes through Italy, Europe, and Latin America."

—VALERIA GALIMI, *Professor of History, University of Florence*

A Brief History of Fascist Lies

A Brief History of
Fascist Lies

Federico Finchelstein

 UNIVERSITY OF CALIFORNIA PRESS

University of California Press
Oakland, California

© 2020, 2022 by Federico Finchelstein
ISBN 978-0-520-38977-9 (pbk.: alk. paper)
ISBN 978-0-520-38978-6 (ebook)

First Paperback Printing 2022

Library of Congress Cataloging-in-Publication Data

Names: Finchelstein, Federico, 1975– author.
Title: A brief history of fascist lies / Federico Finchelstein.
Description: Oakland, California : University of California Press, [2020] |
    Includes bibliographical references and index.
Identifiers: LCCN 2019052243 (print) | LCCN 2019052244 (ebook) |
    ISBN 9780520346710 (cloth) | ISBN 9780520975835 (epub)
Subjects: LCSH: Fascism—History—20th century.
Classification: LCC JC481 .F5177 2020 (print) | LCC JC481 (ebook) |
    DDC 320.53/3—dc23
LC record available at https://lccn.loc.gov/2019052243
LC ebook record available at https://lccn.loc.gov/2019052244

Manufactured in the United States of America

31 30 29 28 27 26 25 24 23 22
10 9 8 7 6 5 4 3 2 1

A Lucia, Gabi, y Laura

Contents

Preface to the Paperback Edition

I started writing this preface in March 2020 in what was then an epicenter of the COVID-19 pandemic. At the time, I was confined to my apartment in New York City, where I have lived and worked for fourteen years, in lockdown. It was a surreal moment and one of the most significant crises of the Trump administration at the end of his first term. Less than two years and a failed coup later, manufactured lies about the virus, vaccines, and the American presidential election of 2020 still occupy center stage.

Writing in this context, I find it regrettable that the history of fascist lies has become an even more pertinent topic today. The history of fascism tells us a great deal about our strange present. The links between past and present suggest that there are convergences in the ways fascist and would-be fascists actors alike deny reality. The extent of the denial sometimes changes reality itself, expanding or even generating disasters.

Lies and Disease

As I discuss in this book, many of the most prominent fascist leaders in history fantasized about creating new realities and ultimately transforming their realities to fit their fantasies. Their successors aspire to do the same. Post-fascists like Donald Trump and his global cronies, including Jair Bolsonaro in Brazil, Viktor Orbán in Hungary, and Narendra Modi in India, exemplify how a crisis unleashed by a pandemic provided an opportunity to channel politics of xenophobia in order to attack democracy. This is not unrelated to strategies of lies and deceit employed by fascists in history. Efforts to blame minority populations and immigrants for the spread of the disease is not new and, in fact, has long been associated with fascism. There are many ways to reduce the transmission of COVID-19, but the combination of political ideology, magic, and bad science is not one of them.

Unfortunately, amid the pandemic, authoritarian ways of combating but really neglecting disease took hold. Political ideology espoused by would-be fascist leaders spread like the virus itself. One must remember that totalitarian ways of dealing with disease did not achieve great results in the past. The fascist mix of political ideologies, racism, and the persecution of otherness did not lead to scientific revolutions or great discoveries but to violence and genocide. During the Holocaust, victims were falsely accused of spreading disease before the Nazis created unsanitary living conditions in ghettos and later in the concentration and extermination camps, where disease ran rampant. Only in a universe created by fascists did the persecuted become ill and eventually spread disease.

More recently, Trump, Bolsonaro, Orbán, and Modi have all lied about the pandemic and used it as an excuse to promote their autocratic will. An emblematic case of these excesses occurred when Trump suggested an "injection" of disinfectant to beat COVID-19 and "clean" the "lungs" while calling for the "liberation" of the people from the basic public health measures that the experts of his own government supported.

After denying the virulence and danger of the virus, Trump's pandemic strategy combined xenophobia and limited public health measures. The American caudillo called COVID-19 the "Chinese virus," a dog whistle with racist undertones, and used the pandemic to promote the construction of his anti-migrant wall, assuring the American public that everything would be fine. Trump pointed fingers at external forces, including China and undocumented migrants, but ignored the viral spread happening among Americans, including his supporters.

Trump was not alone in reassigning blame for an exponentially spreading virus. Modi blamed a group of Muslim missionaries for the spread of the virus without mentioning similar gatherings of Hindu groups. In Orbán's case, the Magyar autocrat used the pandemic to assume quasi-dictatorial authority. In addition to gaining the power to create and cancel laws, Orbán vowed to imprison those who promoted "distorted truths." Another post-fascist liar, Jair Bolsonaro, denied the existence of the disease entirely, rejecting the validity of WHO experts urging stronger public health interventions while the country was slammed with an outbreak early in the pandemic. The same can be said of the post-fascists of the Vox party in Spain or of Matteo Salvini in Italy. All of them blended xenophobic and authoritarian fantasies with dubious understandings of science and disease to the detriment of their supporters and the public at large.

A central element of the fascist lie is projection. Fascists always deny who they are and attribute their own characteristics, their responsibility, and their own totalitarian politics to their enemies. Drawing from this ideological precedent, Trump said on April 27, 2020, "There has been so much unnecessary death in this country. It could have been stopped and it could have been stopped short, but somebody a long time ago, it seems, decided not to do it that way. And the whole world is suffering because of it." Early in the crisis, he promised that the virus would be gone by April, and on February 19, 2020, he told a Phoenix, Arizona, television station, "I think the numbers will get progressively better as we move forward." Four days later, he called the situation "very under control" and added, "We had 12 [positive cases], at one point. And now they have improved a lot. Many of them are fully recovered." By early August 2020, the United States had the highest rate of infection and the most deaths linked to COVID-19 globally. By the beginning of May 2020, almost five million Americans were infected and there were more than 161,000 fatalities. Brazil followed the United States, with almost three million cases and nearly 100,000 deaths. It is no coincidence that the countries with the greatest number of cases and deaths were led by Trump and Bolsonaro: this can be explained, in part, as the result of an authoritarian ideology that denies science and extols lies.

In Brazil, Bolsonaro presented an ideology very close to fascism and mixed with nationalism and the most extreme messianism to ignore the disease and well-being of the population. Worst of all, instead of anticipating the storm, the Brazilian president dedicated himself to promoting it. Specifically, Far Right populisms attack citizens' rights and put the health of the population at greater risk.

Fascistic politics, even when authoritarian leaders are not running the country, have significantly hindered efforts to control the pandemic. In Italy, right-wing populists promoted the idea that the virus was something external to the nation and not a real problem it faced. One leader, Luca Zaia, president of the Veneto region, argued that "the real problem is the media pandemic that they are doing internationally, not the health one."[1] Like Trump and Bolsonaro, the Italian populists denied any responsibility for wrongdoing and even promoted the idea that the virus should be allowed to spread without significant mitigating health measures.

The vice president of the Italian Senate, Ignazio La Russa of the would-be fascist movement Fratelli d'Italia, recommended doing the Fascist salute to avoid contagion, while the French populist leader Marine Le Pen linked freedom of movement within Europe to the propagation of the virus. Once lockdowns and social distancing became the norm, the same leaders opposed these measures in the name of freedom of movement, accusing their government of tyrannical tendencies. This malleability of the truth has key fascist precedents.

Fascists like Hitler typically associated their enemies with lies and disease. They wanted to turn the world upside down, altering what was true and fake. Fascists conceived as lies the facts that ran against their expectations. As we will see in this book, these attempts rested on ideas of the truth that did not need empirical verification.

Replicating the fascist playbook of lies, where the liars accuse others of lying, Le Pen and her associates later accused the French government of lying about the sanitary crisis and argued that she represented "nationalism" against the French government's "globalism."

The idea that the myth of the nation can fight disease has roots in fascism. When nationalist ideology fails to curb a crisis, lies and propaganda increase. Similarly, the Spanish post-fascists of Vox, without real governmental authority, managed to promote propaganda about COVID-19 that contributed to a dire situation. Some Vox leaders became infected after having called for political rallies that drew large crowds and ignored social distancing measures encouraged by public health experts. Once infected, these post-fascists leaned into their xenophobic fantasies to argue that the virus was a Chinese entity and that their antibodies fought China and personified the nation as a whole. For historians of fascism and health, this fusion between national struggle and disease is an indelible quality common to fascist regimes.

The Big Lies about Coups and Elections

The type of distortion of authoritarianism that we are currently witnessing, which also presents itself as a defender of democracy, has a sad history that goes from Hitler, Mussolini, Franco, and Pinochet to Bolsonaro and Trump. In 2019, Bolsonaro celebrated the 1964 coup that led to the military dictatorship in Brazil and claimed that that dictatorship had established democracy.

Trump presented his autocratic plan to reverse the results of the presidential elections through violence exerted by armed citizens as an attempt "to save our democracy." He told his followers before they marched down Pennsylvania Avenue toward the Capitol, "We fight like hell. And if you don't fight like hell, you're not going to have a country anymore."

Amid the collapse of the traditional Latin American, American, and European political elites, these leaders turn elections into plebiscites based on big lies about the functioning of democracy. As the philosopher Hannah Arendt argued, politics and lies always go together, but in fascism lies increase both quantitatively (fascists blatantly lie) and qualitatively (fascists believe their lies and attempt to transform reality to resemble their own lies). In this context, leaders like Bolsonaro, Modi, and many others take up the Trumpist torch and turn their lies into a serious threat to democracy.

Donald Trump lost the American presidential election, but he still preferred to live in an alternate world his own propaganda created. In this bizarre universe, Trump is considered an invincible hero of mythical proportions who decides what is right and what is wrong, what is fake and what is not.

In truth, Trump first lied that he won the election and then denied his undeniable defeat. However, in Trumpworld the defeated still appears as the winner. This fanatic denial of reality is, in a nutshell, a key essence of Trumpism.

We need to understand the conditions that made Trump possible. How did we end up with a right-wing populist who denied science during a pandemic and then denied democratic electoral results, fanaticized his fake victory and reinstatment, and even attempted a failed coup?

What made the Trumpian disaster possible? A key part of the explanation is the power of lies. In short, central to the success of Trumpism is how lies were fabricated, circulated, sold, and bought by so many Americans.

Misinformation will be remembered as the trademark of the history of Trumpism, a movement, regime, and ideology that brought populism extremely close to fascism. There is no question that many Americans shared with Trump an authoritarian personality as the philosopher Theodor Adorno and his colleagues have studied it in the postwar period. But we should not forget that an equally significant lesson to be learned is that Trumpism succeeded because real news has been constantly downplayed in the media by the amplification of government propaganda.

Fascist Propaganda

Before he became a candidate for president, Donald Trump promoted "birtherism," the racist idea that President Barack Obama was not born in the United States, among other conspiracy theories, to present himself as a political player. As president, Trump reached a new level of propaganda manufacture, largely targeting minorities, immigrants, the novel coronavirus, and finally his defeat in the election. His devotion to and promotion of his non-reality brings him close to leaders like Hitler and Mussolini.

This is why, of all the things said about Donald Trump, the comparison to one of the world's most infamous liars, the Nazi propaganda minister Joseph Goebbels, remains the most extreme, and yet the most accurate. The reason for this is simple: Trump's lies make use of fascist propaganda techniques.

In explaining why Donald Trump lies so much, then president-elect Joe Biden resorted to this apt historical comparison. He said that Trump is "sort of like Goebbels" and continued, "You say the lie long enough, keep repeating it, repeating it, repeating it, it becomes common knowledge."[2] Like many historians of fascism and populism, I think Biden made a strong historical point, although as I explain in this book, Goebbels never said that repeating lies was part of his strategy. He, in fact, like Trump, believed in the lies he himself manufactured. Intoxicated by the ideology of his own cult, Trump likely believed that he was immune to the disease and that the election was stolen. To be sure, most politicians lie, but as a political liar Trump plays in a different league.

From a historical perspective, there is no question Trump participates in a tradition of totalitarian lying that has nothing to do with the conventional lies of traditional politicians of both Left and Right.

Trump lies like the leader of a sect. He believes that his lies serve a larger, faith-based truth that he himself personifies. As we see in this book, the history of fascism presents plenty of cases of liars who believed and wanted to change their worlds to conform to their lies.

There is a chronology of totalitarian lying. Fascists increased and mastered the manufacture of lies after years of being in power. The same happened in Trumpism, and the paroxysm of lies reached its climax in the last few days of Trump's presidency. The latest examples, of course, were the lies about fraud, illegal votes, and so forth, but the real news is that Trump was no longer able to manufacture and spread lies from his perch at the White House. And as of now, there is no longer a Trump-centered news cycle.

From Populism to Fascism

In terms of lies, Trump and his cronies represent a new chapter in populism, unmaking its more democratic dimensions and stressing the authoritarian ones. If populism was historically a reformulation of fascism in a democratic key, the Trumpist way of lying is more akin to fascism. Classic populist leaders like Juan Domingo Perón in Argentina or Getulio Vargas in Brazil did not believe their own lies and never denied science, or the results of elections. But for fascists like Hitler, Mussolini, or Goebbels, knowledge was a matter of faith, of deep faith in the myth of the leader.

The fascist idea that the autocrat's greatness can combat all "evils," including disease, diversity, and inconvenient facts, implies that the leader is the owner of the truth and decides when to share it, ignore it, or, worse yet, try to make it a reality. For the faithful, those who believe in the worship of their leaders, these lies are enough.

Dictators and demagogues who deny reality and create governments grounded in falsehoods find it difficult to deal with the concrete consequences of what they deny. In the case of the COVID-19 pandemic, President Trump was exposed to the virus and became critically ill; worse still, his policies and propaganda exposed and killed many others. Historically, fascist leaders and their lies represented a catastrophic symbiosis. But sooner or later, even ardent followers will see their emperors naked. This happened before, and it will happen again. Liars cannot sustain their lies forever. Unfortunately, before the critical undressing of fascist lies, many citizens pay the price.

New York City, September 18, 2021

Introduction

What you're seeing and what you're reading is not what's happening.

DONALD J. TRUMP, 2018

Since then, a struggle between the truth and the lie has been taking place. As always, this struggle will end victoriously for the truth.

ADOLF HITLER, 1941

You must believe me because I have the habit—it is the system of my life—of always and everywhere saying the truth.

BENITO MUSSOLINI, 1924

One of the key lessons of the history of fascism is that racist lies led to extreme political violence. Today lies are back in power. This is now more than ever a key lesson of the history of fascism. If we want to understand our troublesome present, we need to pay attention to the history of fascist ideologues and to how and why their rhetoric led to the Holocaust, war, and destruction. We need history to remind us how so much violence and racism happened in such a short period. How did the Nazis and other fascists come to power and murder millions of people? They did so by spreading ideological lies. Fascist political power was significantly derived from the co-optation of truth and the widespread promulgation of lies.

Today we're seeing an emergent wave of new right-wing populist leaders throughout the world. And much like fascist leaders of the past, a great deal of their political power is derived from questioning reality; endorsing myth, rage, and paranoia; and promoting lies.

In this book, I offer a historical analysis of fascists' use of political lies and their understanding of the truth. This has become a highly relevant question in the present moment, an era that is sometimes described as post-fascist and sometimes as post-truth. The book presents a historical framework for thinking through the history of lying in fascist politics in order to help us think through the use of political lies in the present.

Lying is, of course, as old as politics. Propaganda, hypocrisy, and mendacity are ubiquitous in the history of political power struggles. Hiding the truth in the name of a greater good is a hallmark of most, if not all, histories of politics. Liberals and communists and monarchs, democrats, and tyrants have also lied repeatedly. To be sure, fascists were not the only ones lying in their time, nor are their descendants the only ones lying in ours. Indeed, the German Jewish philosopher Max Horkheimer once observed that the submission of truth to power is at the heart of modernity.[1] But the same argument can be made for ancient times. In more recent history, studying fascist liars should not mean letting liberals, conservatives, and communists off the hook. Indeed, lies and an elastic understanding of the truth are a hallmark of many political movements.[2] But the point I want to make clear in this book is that fascist and now populist liars play in a league of their own.

Fascist lying in politics is not typical at all. This difference is not a matter of degree, even if the degree is significant. Lying is a feature of fascism in a way that is not true of those other political traditions. Lying is incidental to, say, liberalism, in a way that it is not to fascism. And, in fact, when it comes to fascist deceptions, they share few things with others forms of politics in history. They are situated beyond the more traditional forms of political duplicity. Fascists consider their lies to be at the service of simple absolute truths, which are in fact bigger lies. Thus, their lying in politics warrants a history of its own.

. . .

This book addresses the fascist position on truth, which lays the foundations of what became a fascist history of lies. This history still resonates in our present time whenever fascist terrorists, from Oslo to Pittsburgh and from Christchurch to Poway, decide after turning lies into reality to act on them with lethal violence.

At the time I finished this book, a fascist massacred twenty people at a Walmart in El Paso, Texas, in the worst anti-Hispanic attack in the history of the United States. This fascist terrorist invoked a "truth" that has nothing to do with actual history or with reality. In fact, he invoked "the inconvenient truth" in the title of his short manifesto. The killer maintained that his attack was a preemptive action against Hispanic invaders and that "they are the instigators, not me." He was especially concerned about the American-born children of Hispanic immigrants, whom he clearly did not consider real Americans. In doing so, he promoted a vile and racist metric that he, and others, believe should be the standard for determining

American citizenship or legal status. This metric is based on things that never happened: immigrants do not cross the US border with the intention to conquer or contaminate. But this is not what the racist ideology of white supremacy alleges.

Fascist racism itself is based on the lie that humans are hierarchically divided into master races and inferior races. It is based on the purely paranoiac fantasy that the weaker races aim to dominate the superior ones and that this is why the white races need to preemptively defend themselves. These lies led the killer to kill.

There was nothing new in the terrorist's conflation of lies and death or his projection of his racist and totalitarian views onto the intentions of his victims. Fascists had killed many times before in the name of lies masquerading as truths. But in contrast to previous histories of fascism, this time fascists share common goals with populists in power. In other words, their racist views are shared with the leadership at the White House.

Fascism acts from below, but it is legitimized from above. When the Brazilian president Jair Bolsonaro openly denigrates Afro-Brazilians or when the American president Donald J. Trump talks about Mexicans as rapists or an "invasion" arriving in "caravans," they legitimate fascist thinking in some of their political followers. Racist lies, in turn, proliferate in public discourse. As the *New York Times* explained following the El Paso shooting, "At campaign rallies before last year's midterm elections, President Trump repeatedly warned that America was under attack by immigrants heading for the border. 'You look at what is marching up, that is an invasion!' he declared at one rally. 'That is an invasion!' Nine months later, a 21-year-old white man is accused of opening fire in a Walmart in El Paso, killing 20 people and injuring dozens more after writing a manifesto railing against immigration and announcing that 'this attack is a response to the Hispanic invasion of Texas.'"[3]

The same lies that motivated the El Paso killer are at the center of Trumpism and the so-called effort to Make America Great Again. Lying about things that are part of the permanent record has become part of the American president's daily routine. Trump continuously has used specific propaganda techniques, lying without consequence, replacing rational debate with paranoia and resentment, and casting reality itself into doubt.[4] Trump's attacks on the mainstream media and the extensive documented instances where he claims he didn't say something that is in fact in the public record are related to the history of fascist lies analyzed in this book.

Further, the Trump agenda transforms ideological premises, often based in paranoia and fictions about those who are different or feel or behave differently, into actual politics that include adopting racist measures specifically targeting Muslims and Latino immigrants, as well as denigrating black communities, neighborhoods, journalists, and politicians. At the same time, he has defended white nationalist protesters who attended the march in Charlottesville, Virginia, where a counterprotester was murdered.[5] As Ishaan Tharoor explained in the *Washington Post*, "He has stoked white-nationalist grievances among his base while demonizing, belittling or attacking immigrants and minorities. Just in recent weeks, the president launched tirades against minority congresswomen and spoke of the nation's inner cities as zones of 'infestation.' Ahead of the 2018 midterm elections and now, as his reelection campaign gets into full swing, he stirred fear and anger about an 'invasion' of migrants at the U.S.-Mexico border, warning of an existential peril marching into the country."[6]

How is it possible for the White House to promote and provoke acts by fascist terrorists? As I explained in my previous book, *From Fascism to Populism in History,* we are witnessing a new chapter in the history of fascism and populism, two different political ideologies that now share an objective: to foment xenophobia without preventing political violence. Fascist assassins and populist politicians maintain common goals.

In contrast to fascism, populism is an authoritarian understanding of democracy that reworked the legacy of fascism after 1945 in order to combine it with different democratic procedures. After the defeat of fascism, populism emerged as a form of postfascism, which reformulates fascism for democratic times. Another way of putting it: populism is fascism adapted to democracy.

In the United States, it is not surprising that people whose ideology aligns with Trump's might engage in political violence, from harassing immigrants on the streets to sending bombs to individuals Trump labeled "enemies of the people." These forms of political violence occur outside the direction of the US government and its leadership. And yet Trump bears the moral and ethical responsibility for fostering a climate of violence.[7]

This climate of violence is fomented in the name of racist lies that are repackaged as truth.[8] This situation bears a great many similarities to the fascist lying in history. In fact, there are strong historical ties between German and American fascism. The Nazi party admired US racist and segregationist policies during the early twentieth century, modeling its Nuremberg laws on Jim Crow legislation, which formally legalized public racial segregation.[9] Hitler himself admired stories by the German writer Karl May about the Aryan conquest of the American West. Today Hitler's ideology is echoed in the American neo-Nazis' belief that they are inheritors of the Aryan legacy and responsible for defending it against an invasion.

With the benefit of history, we know that fascist lying had horrible consequences. We know what happened when fascist lies were transformed into reality. It was not only people who supported Hitler's racist policies that made German fascism successful but also people who simply did not care that a defining element of National Socialism was racism. The key difference between then and now is that there is a great deal of condemnation of the president's racist lies and their impact on broad sectors of American society. In contrast to the dictatorial times of Hitler and Mussolini when the free press was eliminated, today the independent press continues to work in the United States. Its task is essential for democracy. Accusing the media of lying, of being untrustworthy, relies on the idea analyzed in this book that only the leader can be the source of truth. In a time when the American president demonizes journalists, even calling them "enemies of the people," the independent press continues to report the lies and corroborate the facts.

This is not only an American story. In Brazil, Bolsonaro, who is called "the Trump of the Tropics," has similarly demonized journalists, glorified the country's dictatorial policies, and subscribed to despicable lies about the environment. Against the facts of climate change, both Trump and Bolsonaro have supported fabrications that are directly linked to one of the biggest crimes on the planet now—the rapid destruction of the Amazon. As with fascist lies about "blood and soil," populist falsehoods are tied to violence not only against people but also against the earth. As *The Guardian* reported, the Amazon forest "is being burned and chopped down at the most alarming rate in recent memory[,] . . . [a]t a clearance rate equivalent to a Manhattan island every day." Bolsonaro denied the facts about the exponential increase in deforestation under his rule and accused his own state agency of providing "false figures." As the *New York Times* reported, "That claim was unfounded."[10]

As the history of fascism demonstrates, questioning these lies is of key importance to the survival of democracy. The fact that Trump is stoking suspicion of our electoral system without real evidence should not be taken lightly. For example, he claimed that millions of undocumented people in California voted for Hillary Clinton in 2016 and that election fraud existed in other states—claims that he himself could not prove. These and other recurrent examples of Trumpist lying stand as serious attacks on democracy. They do so in a manner that unsettles faith in democratic institutions just as the fascists did. However, a key difference, so far, is that populists merely want to diminish the power of representative democracy, whereas fascists wanted to end democracy. Today we know that democracy needs to be actively defended because democratic institutions and traditions are not as strong as many believe them to be. Indeed, lies can destroy democracy.

The aim of this book is to understand why twentieth-century fascists regarded simple, often hateful lies as truth and why others believed them. Historically, lies have been the starting point of undemocratic politics, a fact that had disastrous consequences for fascism's victims. For this reason alone, the history of lying cannot be excluded from the inquiries of historians of modern political violence, racism, and genocide.

The prominent fascist leaders of the twentieth century—from Mussolini to Hitler—regarded lies as the truth incarnate in themselves. This stood at the center of their notions of power, popular sovereignty, and history. An alternate universe where truth and falsehood cannot be distinguished rests on the logic of myth.[11] In fascism, mythical truth replaced factual truth.

In the present, lies again seem to increasingly replace empirical truth. As facts are presented as "fake news" and ideas originating among those who deny the facts become government policy, we must remember that current talk about "post-truth" has a political and intellectual lineage: the history of fascist lying.

1   On Fascist Lies

I punched some of those precise liars in the face. The witnesses approved my relief, and fabricated other lies. I didn't believe them, but I didn't dare to ignore them.

JORGE LUIS BORGES

The most famous fascist propagandist, the Nazi leader Joseph Goebbels, is often misquoted as saying that repeating lies was central to Nazism. This misquotation has led to an image of a fascism fully conscious of the extent of its deliberate falsehoods.[1] Is deception at the center of fascism? Do liars believe their own lies? Are they cognizant of falsity? When Goebbels said that Hitler knew everything, and that he was a "[t]he naturally creative instrument of divine destiny,"[2] did he actually have a reality-based notion of knowledge?

This is complicated. In fact, having once faked and then published news about an assassination attempt on himself, Goebbels then "published" it as fact in his diaries. In these diaries, not written for public consumption but published many years after his death, he also noted the "success" of his speeches after they were celebrated by the media he controlled.[3] Was Goebbels lying to himself, or did he believe in a form of truth that transcended empirical demonstration? Did he want to fabricate a new reality? Of course, from a reality-based perspective, there is no difference between the fabrication of a lie and the belief in a magical idea of truth, an escape from veracity. By inventing an alternative reality, Goebbels was lying to himself, but this is not what he and most transnational fascists believed.

For fascists like Goebbels, knowledge was a matter of faith, and especially a deep faith in the myth of the fascist leader. The manipulation or the invention of facts was a key dimension of fascism, but so was a belief in a truth that transcended facts. Fascists did not see a contradiction between truth and propaganda.

Goebbels defined propaganda as "the art, not of lying or distorting, but of listening to 'the soul of the people' and 'speaking to a person a language that this person understands.'" As Richard Evans, the historian, observes, "The Nazis acted on the premise that they, and they alone, through Hitler, had an inner knowledge and understanding of the German soul."[4] The idea of a truth that emanated from the soul was the result of an act of faith in an absolute certainty that could not be corroborated.

When Adolf Hitler talked about big lies and big truths, this was symptomatic of his work to upend the world of true and fake. What this man understood as lies were facts that ran against his racist theory of the universe. His conception of the world rested on a notion of truth that did not need empirical verification. In other words, what is truth for most of us (the result of demonstrable causes and effects) was potentially fake for him. What most of us would see as lies or invented facts were for him superior forms of truth. Much like current populist media claims today, Hitler inverted reality by projecting onto his enemies his own dishonesty regarding the truth, falsely stating that the Jews were liars, not him. The fascist liar acted as if he represented the truth. He accused Jews of engaging in "colossal distortion of the Truth." But Hitler identified this real truth with the anti-Semitic myths that he believed and propagated.

The foremost connoisseurs of this truth regarding the possibilities in the use of falsehood and slander have always been the Jews; for after all, their whole existence is based on the great lie, to wit, that they are a religious community while actually they are a race—and what a race! One of the greatest minds of humanity has nailed them forever as such in an eternally correct phrase of fundamental truth: he called them 'the great masters of the lie'. And anyone who does not recognize this or does not want to believe it will never in this world be able to help the truth to victory.[5]

In the 1930s and 1940s, Hitler, the Argentine fascists, and many other fascists around the world saw truth embodied in anti-Semitic myths—what the German Jewish philosopher Ernst Cassirer called "myth according to plan."[6] Fascists fantasized a new reality and then changed the actual one. Thus, they redrew the frontiers between myth and reality. Myth replaced reality with policies aimed at reshaping the world according to the lies racists believed. If anti-Semitic lies stated that Jews were inherently dirty and contagious and therefore ought to be killed, the Nazis created conditions in the ghettos and concentration camps where dirtiness and widespread disease became reality. Starved, tortured, and radically dehumanized Jewish inmates became what the Nazis had planned for them to become, and were accordingly killed.

In their search for a truth that did not coincide with the experienced world, fascists resorted to making metaphors reality. There was nothing true about fascist ideological falsehoods, but their adherents nonetheless wanted to make these lies real enough. They conceived what they saw and did not like as *untruth*. Mussolini argued that a core task of fascism was to deny the lies of the democratic system. He also opposed the truth of fascism to the "lie" of democracy. The principle of incarnation was central to il Duce's mythical opposition between democratic "lies" and fascist "truth." He believed in a form of truth that transcended democratic common sense because it was transcendental. He recalled, "At a certain moment in my life I risked being unpopular with the masses to announce to them what I thought was the new truth, a holy truth [*la verità santa*]".[7]

For Mussolini, reality had to follow mythical imperatives. Too bad if people were not initially convinced; their disbelief also needed to be challenged. The mythical framework of fascism was rooted in the fascist myth of the nation. This myth, he declared, "we wish to translate into a complete reality." Myth could change reality; reality, however, could not represent an obstacle to myth. This sacred truth of fascism was equally defined by the imposition of peculiar boundaries between fascist truths and the fake nature of the enemy. On the other side, there were the lies of the enemy. Across European borders, people were enchanted by "the obsession of the Russian Myth"—Bolshevism—but Mussolini considered that these rival myths were false insofar as they opposed the absolute forms of Truth rooted in extreme nationalism, and of course his own leadership, which he had identified with myth.[8] To that myth, the Duce said, "we subordinate all the rest."[9]

In their modernization of myth, fascists turned it from a matter of personal belief to a primary form of political identification. In this reformulation, true politics was the projection of an ancient and violent inner self that overcame the artifices of reason when it was applied to politics. This operation allowed them to define as true everything that conformed to their own ideological aims, postulates, and desires.

This mythic dimension of fascism was antidemocratic. Democracy has historically rested on notions of truth as the opposite of lies, mistaken beliefs, and erroneous information.[10] In contrast, fascists presented a radical notion of truth in dictatorship. As the historian Robert Paxton explained, for fascists, "the truth was whatever permitted the new fascist man (and woman) to dominate others, and whatever made the chosen people triumph. Fascism rested not upon the truth of its doctrine but upon the leader's mystical union with the historic destiny of his people, a notion related to romanticist ideas of national historic flowering and of individual artistic or spiritual genius, though fascism otherwise denied romanticism's exaltation of unfettered personal creativity."[11]

Fascists' metaphorical unification of people, nation, and leader rested on seeing myth as the ultimate form of truth. But there were many political precedents. This uncanny status of truth and lies in fascism is a recurring dimension of the long history of the relationship between truth and politics. For the philosopher Hannah Arendt, if the history of politics always demonstrates a tense relationship with truth, the fascist resolution of this tension implies the destruction of politics. Organized lying defines fascism. Only facts (and lies) prescribed by the leadership could be accepted as truth.

The distortion of truth in the name of promoting an alternate reality is a phenomenon common in fascist history. The Spanish fascist dictator Francisco Franco famously denied his role in one of his greatest war crimes: the gruesome bombing of Guernica that left hundreds dead. Though the bombing was a well-documented act of the fascist government, Franco claimed that "the Reds" had "destroyed Guernica" in order to spread "propaganda" and lies about him. [12] In doing so, he co-opted the very notion of truth, claiming that the lies were not his but those of his political enemies.

In this same sense, Nazis did not distinguish between observable facts and ideologically driven "truths." The most radical outcome of totalitarian dictatorship emerged when "mass leaders seize[d] the power to fit reality to their lies."[13] Some years later, in her controversial study of Adolf Eichmann, Arendt provided a major inquiry into the reasoning of one planner of the Holocaust who epitomized this phenomenon of "extreme contempt for fact as such." Arendt equated Eichmann's subscription to lies with an entire society "shielded against reality and factuality by exactly the same means, the same self-deception, lies, and stupidity that had now become engrained in Eichmann's mentality."[14]

Arendt missed an important dimension of the Eichmann trial: the perspective of the truth as presented by the victims.[15] Also missing in Arendt's portrayal of Eichmann is the man's deep ideological dedication, even fanaticism. Even at the moment of his death, Eichmann ceremoniously stated, "Long live Germany, long live Argentina, long live Austria. I shall not forget them."[16] Arendt identifies this moment as one of "grotesque silliness," an elation as Eichmann sensed the relevance of his own death. But for Arendt this realization suggested a formulaic representation of the moment rather than its ideological understanding. She identified Eichmann's last words with "clichés" and the banality of evil. Other historians have preferred to emphasize how this choice of last words, and more generally his Nazi past and crimes, was the result of Eichmann's deep commitment to what he regarded as the essential ideological truth of Nazism.[17] Eichmann saw his life and death as a memory that went beyond his multicity transatlantic itinerary, from Berlin to Buenos Aires and from Buenos Aires to Jerusalem.

Many years before Eichmann met justice in Jerusalem, the Argentine writer Jorge Luis Borges imagined a similar Nazi death in a story published in Buenos Aires in 1946. After the defeat of Nazism, Borges's fictional killer, Otto Dietrich zur Linde, reflects on the meaning of fascism, the past and the present. Zur Linde had lived the sublime moment of war, but for him it was in defeat that the definitive truth would be fully revealed: in "the great days and nights of a happy war. In the very air we breathed there was a feeling not unlike love. As though the sea were suddenly nearby, there was wonder and an exultation in the blood." But truth had not been found in this exaltation. It was not in the sublime moment of victory but in the flavor of the "excrement" of defeat that Nazis like himself found a truth that transcended factual explanations.

I thought I was emptying the cup of anger, but in the excrements I encountered an unexpected flavor, the mysterious and almost terrible flavor of happiness. I essayed several explanations, but none seemed adequate. I thought: I am pleased with defeat, because secretly I know I am guilty, and only punishment can redeem me. I thought: I am pleased with defeat because it is an end and I am very tired. I thought: I am pleased with defeat because it has occurred, because it is irrevocably united to all those events which are, which were, and which will be, because to censure or to deplore a single real occurrence is to blaspheme the universe. I played with these explanations, until I found the true one.

After discarding facts and lived experience, zur Linde circularly identified truth with the Nazi faith. For zur Linde, subdirector of the Tarnowitz concentration camp, the true "explanation" of fascism rested on the affirmation of the devotion to violence. This was a faith—not needing corroboration—that would establish "heaven" on earth: "The world was dying of Judaism, and of that disease of Judaism that is the faith of Jesus; we taught it violence and the faith in the sword."[18]

As Borges playfully suggested in the quotation that serves as the epigraph of this chapter, one should recognize lies as such, but one cannot afford to ignore them when analyzing the acts of violence they inspire. Even if it is clear to us that, like Borges's imaginary Nazi narrator, Eichmann was deceiving himself in Jerusalem, this is not how fascists explained and lived their actions. The fascists' way of understanding their role in history in mythical terms demands a historical explanation. Arendt was keen to point to the function and role of these lies in the totalitarian system without analyzing why fascists believed in them in the first place. She was not that interested in the rationale for their motives. Arendt argued, "The ideal subject of totalitarian rule is not the convinced Nazi or the convinced Communist, but people for whom the distinction between fact and fiction (i.e., the reality of experience) and the distinction between true and false (i.e., the standards of thought) no longer exist."[19] But as important as this "ideal" general subject is, in this book my focus is on those who were convinced. In other words, Arendt was dealing with ideal types, and I look at actual, historically documented figures, empirically grounding my arguments in the history of fascism. Historians of fascism also need to understand how fascists justified their lies.

Why did fascists believe their lies to be the truth? As many anti-fascists noted at the time, the fascist history of dictatorship was founded on lies. The mythical imaginary the fascists put forward as reality could never be corroborated because it was based on fantasies of total domination in the past and present. Thus, this book presents the history of lies in fascism.

2 Truth and Mythology in the History of Fascism

In 1945, Hannah Arendt observed that fascism was an absolute lie, a lie with horrific political effects. Fascists deliberately transformed lies into reality. "The essential thing was that they exploited the age-old Occidental prejudice which confuses reality with truth," she wrote, "and made that 'true' which until then could only be stated as a lie."

For Arendt, reality is malleable, changeable, but truth is not. For her, any argument with fascists was meaningless. In fact, fascists acted to give their "lies" a "post facto basis in reality"— effectively destroying truth, not hiding it. In Arendt's view, this form of ideological politics inexorably leads to the obliteration of reality as we know it. Fascist lies produced an alternative reality. But Arendt's own interpretation would suggest that the destruction of truth was fueled by a belief in what the fascists understood as a more transcendental truth rather than a simple lie.[1] Arendt was not simply insulting fascists. Like her, many antifascist contemporaries wanted to understand why so many people were persuaded that fascist ideology represented a single truth. To be sure, some prominent fascists were hypocrites and liars who conceived of ideology as a tool for propaganda. But if so, why and how did their most important leaders and many of their adherents often follow these lies and propaganda to the end, to the point that they died for their cause? Who dies for a lie?

Fascism was not a simple and hypocritical lie but a lived and believed experience both from above and from below. The creation of a fascist self through the internalization of fascist themes had multiple meanings, official ones as well as spontaneous instances of fascist perception.[2] There were many believers. In fascism, fiction displaced reality and *became* a reality. For nonbelievers, these fascist fantasies could and can only be considered false positions, inauthentic claims on the nature of politics. The opposite is true for the fascists.

Notably, in the period between 1922 and 1945 there was an extraordinary consensus among fascists and antifascists regarding the nonrational nature of transcendental truth in fascism and regarding the pertinence of the unconscious in politics. For the fascists, the unconscious—a complex term used by Sigmund Freud, Theodor W. Adorno, and others to convey the most irrational dimension of the self, the part that was incapable of consciousness—simply represented the prerational inner self that fascism would make conscious.

In contrast to Freud and psychoanalysts more generally, fascists developed an idea of this self as a source of truth, a state of preconsciousness that fascism could draw from and translate into political reality. As we will see, fascists, but also many others, often used this idea of the self to highlight the fact they understood themselves as the primary interpreters of subconscious political imperatives that at times transcended their own nations and crisscrossed the globe. In fascism, the move from unconsciousness to consciousness represented the moment when transcendental truth was finally revealed.

In historical terms, fascism can be defined as a global ideology with national movements and regimes. Fascism was a transnational phenomenon both inside and outside Europe. A modern counterrevolutionary formation, it was ultranationalist, antiliberal, and anti-Marxist. Fascism, in short, was not a mere reactionary position. Its primary aim was to destroy democracy from within in order to create a modern dictatorship from above.

It was the product of a crisis of capitalism and a concurrent crisis of democratic representation. Transnational fascists proposed a totalitarian state in which plurality and civil society would be silenced and there would increasingly be no distinctions between the public and the private, or between the state and its citizens. In fascist regimes, the independent press was shut down and the rule of law entirely destroyed.

Fascism defended a divine, messianic, and charismatic form of leadership that conceived of the leader as organically linked to the people and the nation. It considered popular sovereignty to be fully delegated to the dictator, who acted in the name of the community of the people and knew better than they what they truly wanted. Fascists replaced history and empirically based notions of truth with political myth. They had an extreme conception of the enemy, regarding it as an existential threat to the nation and to its people that had to be first persecuted and then deported or eliminated. Fascism aimed to create a new and epochal world order through an incremental continuum of extreme political violence and war. A global ideology, fascism constantly reformulated itself in different national contexts and underwent constant national permutations.

Fascism was officially founded in Italy in 1919, but the politics it represented appeared simultaneously across the world. From Japan to Brazil and Germany and from Argentina to India and

France, the antidemocratic, violent, and racist revolution of the Right that fascism represented was adopted in other countries under different names: Nazism in Germany, *nacionalismo* in Argentina, *integralismo* in Brazil, and so on. Fascism was transnational even before Mussolini used the word *fascismo*, but when fascism became a regime in Italy in 1922, the word received worldwide attention and acquired different meanings in local contexts. This is not to say that the Italian (or the French or later the German) influences were not important for transnational fascists.

Fascists combined various short-term strategies with a long-standing basic preconception of the world. The fascist synthesis was based on this impossible transition from the politics of daily life to dogma. Fascist interpreters across the world had to articulate the often-tense relationship between fascist practice (strategy) and ideal (theory). Ideas about the divine, race, the people, empire, and a mythical past were constantly adapted to the particularities of the very different realities of East and Southeast Asia, Europe, the Middle East, and Latin America. In India and the Middle East, fascist ideas served the purpose of rethinking an authoritarian variant of postcolonialism, whereas in Japan they were used to rethink the modernity of the empire. In republican, postcolonial Latin America, fascism often presented itself as having continuities with the prerepublican Spanish empire but also as the primary way of advancing an authoritarian form of anti-imperialism. Above all fascism developed a radical form of political subjectivity. Fascism's inner meaning represented the fascist matrix, its sacred founding dimension. This conception of an unconscious, prerational intuition expressed the supposed purity of the fascist ideal, the "fascist feeling" that kept the fascist universes of people and specific ideas tied together.

Fascism was formulated on the basis of a modern idea of popular sovereignty but one in which political representation was eliminated and power was fully delegated to the dictator, who acted in the name of the people. Mythical ideas legitimized the fascist order of things and were regarded as transcendental truths.[3]

Fascism's equation of power, myth, and truth was not entirely new. For critical antifascists, fascism followed and transformed a long-standing tradition of unreason. Perspicacious observers among them noted that important romantic traditions functioned as a background to the fascist notion of truth, a "reality" that emerged in and out of the self. Remarkably, during the interwar years, the Argentine writer Jorge Luis Borges called attention to the work of Thomas Carlyle—the Scottish historian, satirist, and enemy of Progressivism— as the intellectual precursor of fascism. For Borges, Carlyle was "a dreamer of nightmares." He proposed a "political theory" that his contemporaries misunderstood "but now fits in a single and quite divulged word: Nazism." This genealogy of fascism suggested a world where "heroes were intractable semi-gods that, not without military frankness and bad words, ruled a subaltern humanity."[4]

If Borges emphasized the peculiar contributions of European writers and philosophers, he neglected to mention converging intellectual genealogies of fascism in his own Latin American context. In the critical writings on liberalism of José Enrique Rodó, the Uruguayan author of *Ariel,* which launched the preeminent form of Latin American romanticism, and in the early work of Leopoldo Lugones, Argentina's most famous writer at the time, we find a notion of truth that emerged from the self and was imbued with a plain sense of beauty and order.

An earlier Latin American romantic tradition had emphasized a connection between liberalism and the construction of an autonomous self open to dissent, questioning the contradictions of the outside world. Rodó and Lugones identified these contradictions with modern liberal democracies. Earlier anti-individualist antidemocratic thinkers, from the positivist Auguste Comte to the anti-Enlightenment reactionary Joseph de Maistre, devised the idea of the need for an absolute truth in politics.[5] Rodó and Lugones followed suit.

The rejection of existing democracy was at the center of these writers' mystical calls for a return to classical Greece. For Rodó and the early Lugones (in his socialist and liberal-conservative phases, which preceded his fascist turn of the 1920s), defining the basic intellectual genealogy of the continent, the classical legacy, allowed Latin American nations to bypass modern Europe and the United States. As an interwar fascist, Lugones would return to these views of Argentina and Latin America. He saw his country and continent as emanations of the classic myths that called the basic tenets of reason and modernity into question. For him, the return of myth prefigured what he would call the "truthful creation" of dictatorship.[6]

While fascists like Lugones created a mythical past for their modern proposal for fascist dictatorship, Borges shared with many other transatlantic antifascists a more critical historical understanding of fascism's origins in anti-Enlightenment ideology. In 1934, Max Horkheimer argued that "the tendency to subordinate the truth to power did not first emerge with fascism." Irrationalism "pervades the entire history of the modern era and limits its concept of reason."[7] Similarly, writing at the end of World War II, Ernst Cassirer stressed that the idea that "truth lies in power" went back to Hegel and presented "the clearest and most ruthless program of fascism."[8] For these antifascist authors, fascism was the symptom of an irrational mythical tradition (Horkheimer) and its novelty was a "technique" that produced terrible effects and affected the course of nature (Cassirer). Arendt, like Borges before her, stressed that fascist ideas of power led to novel forms of conceptual and practical dehumanization. This became possible because fascism stood against equality in interpretation. It rejected the idea of universally shared reason as the sole criterion for telling the truth. Fascism established a variety of mythical lineages that were, for it, the ultimate source of what was politically truthful. Fascism blurred the divide between true and false in politics. Fascism produced a "truth" that was nationalistic and at the same time absolute. Devoid of plural connotations, truth excluded any form of dissent and became the exclusive outcome of hierarchical power relations.

By questioning rational definitions of truth, fascists insisted on the hidden meaning of truth. For them, truth was a secret revealed in and through power. In fascism power acquired a fully transcendental status. For fascists what was powerful, and violent and potent, was truthful and legitimate because it was the expression of transhistorical, mythical trends about the people and the nation. As a living myth that encompassed both, the leader represented the actualization of these trends in power. Power derived from the affirmation of myth through violence, destruction, and conquest.

As a result, fascist politics was mythology. In fascism, the ultimate form of truth required no corroboration with empirical evidence: rather, it emanated from an intuitive affirmation of notions that were supposed to be expressions of transhistorical myths. The leader embodied these myths. This dissociation of political analysis from reality was a fateful development, an outcome of fascism's search for an ultimate form of political authenticity that could transcend reason. In this sense, fascists were not merely lying, but self-deceiving. They fell, as Adorno suggested in 1951, under the fascist "spell" of "untruth." He argued, "The continuous danger of war inherent in Fascism spells destruction and the masses are at least preconsciously aware of it. Thus, Fascism does not altogether speak the untruth when it refers to its own irrational powers, however faked the mythology which ideologically rationalizes the irrational may be."[9]

Similarly, for Arendt, totalitarian ideology takes some elements from reality but leads to empirical blindness. Historically, this ideological operation led to the conflation of reality and fantasy. The belief in lies was part of the education of totalitarian followers, and especially the elites, who turned "ideological lies" into "sacred untouchable truths."[10]

But did fascists believe their lies just because they were voiced by leaders? Or did they rather regard them as more veritable forms of truth emerging from the inner self? For the fascist, these were not contradictory possibilities. Here lies the ideological nature of the fascist notion of truth. Fascism identified truth with a transcendental myth rooted in the collective unconscious and then realized by and through the consciousness of the leader. This belief in the externalization, the "outing," of the unconscious was central to fascists. In fascism, collective desires were thought to be present in the body and speech of the leader. The leader was expected to make conscious what was supposedly genuinely unconscious, and thus authentic and truthful.

3 Fascism Incarnate

Fascism proposed the notion of truth that transcended reason and was incarnated in the myth of the leader. The myth was literally embodied in the person of the leader. For fascists, incarnation was the opposite of representation. In fascist ideology, language could not represent the reality of inner feelings insofar as generic conceptions implied a rational process of translation. Only images or actions, not self-reflective thoughts or the words they expressed, could instantiate and put those feelings into practice. For fascists, this was the essence of fascism's authenticity in politics. They stood above all against reason and believed themselves to be firmly rooted in the mythical. The origins of fascism cannot be understood through the "cold calculus of reason." Fascism was "nontheoretical and nonlogical." It was "an instinctive reaction."[1] Fascism was a recurrent fantasy that by changing reality became reality. In this specific sense, it was an intellectual revolution. The fascist revolution became this attempt to actualize, to objectify, the instinctual forces of desire in the political sphere. On an epistemological level, this attempt engaged fascism in a constant refusal to recognize the humanistic tenets of perception.

Fascism stressed the power of intuition over self-reflection. Here the notion of civilizational transformation on a global scale was central. Fascism saw itself as a transnational ideology that opposed the putative barbarism of liberalism. In contrast with the influential Crocean notion of fascism as a "national parenthesis" that had nothing to do with national culture, the fascists defined their national traditions as emanating from a specific national self rooted in the souls of individuals.[2] In this context, only fascism represented the true intuitive nature of nationalism; liberalism, on the other hand, was an artificial form of conceiving the nation.

This idea was exemplified in and through the sacred incarnation of the leader and the nation in the body of the leader. As the historian Dominick LaCapra argues, this notion has a deep religious background in the theological "idea of full incarnation of divinity in the world."[3] Even in death, the leader lived in the bodies of others, as he had incarnated the sacred in the world. His words remained the truth. As the Romanian fascist leader Horia Sima stated in 1940, regarding the assassinated Romanian leader Captain Corneliu Codreanu, the "thought and the will of the greatest leader of our lineage" was going to help them realize a new man, an authentic elite, "and a country like the sacred sun of heaven." His word was "the torch of boundless love of the Captain for us. It is law for the centuries for the Romanian lineage. His salute remains unchanged, because we want to grow in His spirit. Until the Romanian sky does not get dark over our spirits, the Captain cannot die. We have it among us, he lives among us."[4]

The recognition of the leader as a transcendental figure mirrored the elevation of obedience to a national community of unified wills.[5] The leader ideally expressed this collective will. Engagement in a "ritual" organized the life of the individual in an organic way. The personal submission to the "myth" and hierarchy of movement, party, and state implied the recognition of the individual's role in the chain of links that would lead to the creation of a new reality, and this reality then adapted the world to the ideological imperatives of the myth. As the fascist intellectual Camillo Pellizzi saw it, there was a quasi-unconscious dimension to the fascist attempt to create a new world.[6]

Like reality, the past itself needed to be changed to accord with ideological imperatives. It had to be rewritten in the logic of absolute truth. As the Mexican fascist José Vasconcelos wrote about the politics of history of the Argentine fascists, "In Argentina a Spanish and Catholic nationalist movement is developing. . . . [T]hey are now writing Argentine history upside down, that is, according to the truth, rectifying all the lies of liberalism."[7] The fascist view of history often regarded the historical as a site of contention, a malleable adversary to be defeated and then corrected.[8] Enemies and events were not true subjects in the sense that they did not embody authentic national potency as it was supposedly emerging from the fascist unconscious and as it was embodied in the leader.

On a superficial level fascism belonged to history. As the fascist writer Volt maintained, as a "historical fact" fascism did not differ from other political formations. It was a historical event within the chain of facts, laws, and institutions. As a fact, fascism belonged to a political chronology. But on a deeper level, that is, as an idea, fascism was "anti-historical." It defied the logic of facts that change over time. In this sense, Volt argued, fascism was not historical. If history was a narrative, fascism was a principle. The task of fascists was to apply this principle to the changing circumstances. They wanted to impose fascism on the historical narrative. "As a principle the fascist truth is immutable, eternal," Volt wrote.⁹ This immutable truth existed as an absolute form of inner recognition: "For fascism . . . the absolute exists. . . . It is that which justifies its existence, which sanctifies its action."¹⁰

The truth could only be an authentic expression of ideology, and especially the ideas of the leaders. The notion of a mythical truth incarnated in the leader was certainly not European but a mark of transnational fascism. In Peru, fascists stated in 1934 that their "Supreme Leader of the Party," Luis Flores, "has grasped the desires and just social and economic aspirations of the majority of citizens. These yearnings are incarnated in the true nationalist spirit of the Peruvian workers . . . and the high principles of the most authentic nationalism."¹¹ Authenticity was not the result of demonstration but the affirmation of a sacred essence.

In India, the Indo-Muslim fascist Inayatullah Khan al-Mashriqi presented a superior form of truth that only his leadership could reveal: "the Qur'an that can, if at all, only be put together only in those minds who have got to see every nook and corner of this magnificent cosmos, who have acquired substantial knowledge of the mysteries of the Book of Nature, who have been elevated by the majestic heights of knowledge and the grand vistas of ultimate reality to the higher horizon of the heavens and the stars; who, unperturbed by the technicalities of lowly logic, are pursuing the finality of absolute truth."¹²

Incarnation was the means to acquiring ultimate truth. The leader and his followers were supposed to embody historical and mythical figures. While Japanese fascists wanted to imagine an imperial "restoration" of the past that combined populist-sounding themes and appeal with the idea of a transhistorical *kokutai* (national polity), Egyptian fascists linked themselves with the traditions of Pharaonic Egypt.¹³

In Japan, the emperor represented a patriarchal figure, and fascists wanted to eradicate parliamentary institutions that impeded more direct connections between the sovereign and the people. The totalitarian embodiment of this mythical link between past and present was organically rooted in truth. People and state were amalgamated in the imperial institution, which according to myth had been unbroken for thousands of years. As a Japanese fascist argued, "In the case of Japan and the Japanese, totalitarianism is for the first time not just reckless talk but an embodiment of reality."[14]

In Egypt, the fascist leader of the Green Shirts, Ahmad Husayn, argued in 1935, "Nature teaches us that there can be no accord between the ruler and the ruled, nor between the strong and the weak. Agreement can only be reached by struggle and strife. The conqueror is the worthy one because he continues to exist; the conquered is weak, so he is exterminated."[15] In the incarnated leader fascists saw a truth that transcended facts, but they (or he) also manipulated the facts to create a more elevated truth. This was ideological truth in the form of revelation. If the leader embodied what was eternally true, fascists concluded that his critics were liars. They considered them enemies of the truth.

4 Enemies of the Truth?

Hitler famously wrote, "Hence today I believe that I am acting in accordance with the will of the Almighty Creator: *by defending myself against the Jew, I am fighting for the work of the Lord.*"[1] This Nazi idea of action as the practical consequence of God's desires resulted in the invention, persecution, and elimination of enemies that Hitler identified with untruth. Likewise, in Argentina clerico-fascist intellectuals linked the lies of anti-Semitism to the eternal truths of the sacred. And they also believed and promoted the fake notion of a Jewish race. Not unlike Hitler, they asserted the veracity of these lies as emanations of Christian truths.

Hitler became a living god for the Nazis, embarking on a collision course with the Christian churches. In Latin America, the leader never quite replaced God. There, the relationship between official religion and the sacred truth of fascism was much more harmonious. For fascists, confirming Catholicism as a transcendental truth depended on affirming the lies of anti-Semitism. In the Jews they saw a living confirmation of battles that transcended human history.

José Vasconcelos was perhaps the most important intellectual of the Mexican Revolution. Vasconcelos opposed the "hidden plans" of Judaism to "the light of the truth."[2] He famously proposed a "cosmic race" that would integrate its European and Indian heritages. Vasconcelos eventually became rector of the Universidad Nacional Autónoma de México (UNAM), Mexico's national university, and then secretary of education. After being defeated in the presidential elections of 1929, he went into exile. There, and especially during his years in Argentina, he turned to the Right and denounced embracing their native legacy as a suicidal choice for Latin Americans. Only the Hispanic, Mediterranean, and Catholic heritages could define the Latin American self. In 1933 in Argentina, he declared that "the Mexican revolution is an authentic filth [*cochinada*]." By the late 1930s he had embraced fascism, which in the Mexican context also meant a repudiation of the most secular dimensions of the revolution.[3]

Like his peers in Argentina, Vasconcelos became an idiosyncratic clerico-fascist. He believed that the Jews wanted to use lies to destroy Christian civilization. Reason and history were not going to provide the answer. Truth would be found elsewhere. In an article published in Vasconcelos's fascist magazine, *Timón,* the Mexican fascist Fernando de Euzcadi argued, "We let ourselves be fooled by that juggling of reasons and we slip through the dangerous inclined plane of History looking in it for a justification for what is only a consequence of our cowardice and a renunciation of our more valued feelings." Feelings could reveal the conspiracy of the Jews, who were the "true dictators of our lives and lock our consciences." According to de Euzcadi, all Jewish activities were untruthful, marked by "the pirouette of the farce."[4]

Like the Mexican fascists, Hitler believed in his own propaganda and projected his own actions (i.e., spreading lies) onto the Jews. He described Jews as the best propaganda men. The "Jew" was "the great master of lies."[5] Similarly, Argentine fascists invoked God to justify their anti-Semitic fantasies and paranoia. This led them to spread lies about Jewish life in Argentina and the world. While Fr. Virgilio Filippo falsely proposed that the Jews aimed to model Argentina after themselves, Fr. Julio Meinvielle spuriously ascribed to them conquering intentions and argued that the Argentine battle against the Jews was related to the transhistorical fight of "biblical peoples" for the "conquest of the world." Meinvielle talked about the dangerous features of the "mixture between Jews and Christians," while Filippo warned bluntly of the need to limit the influence of an invasive "race" continuously preoccupied with its racial purity.

In contrast to Hitler, the Argentine fascists believed the ultimate leader of their movement was Jesus Christ.[6] But like Hitler, Filippo and others projected their own racial bias onto his victims and claimed that the Jews were clearly concerned with their own "racial prophylaxis." Filippo believed that fighting the Jews meant exposing "Jewish racism." This line of argument downplayed the traditional objections of religious anti-Semitism and suggested a higher racial truth: "It is not true that the Jews constitute in the first place a religious community. They are a race."[7] Conforming to common belief at the time, Filippo assumed that certain specific physiological traits made Jewish bodies visible and recognizable. His Jewish stereotype coincided with many other European stereotypes.[8] For anti-Semites and fascists worldwide, anti-Semitism acted as a cultural code, a repertoire of racist fantasies shared across borders and adapted to different nations. Fascists used this catalog of lies and prejudices to read between the lines of what seemed difficult to understand and reduced the complexity of the world by adhering to what they believed was a higher truth. As the historian Simon Levis Sullam explained, fascists resorted to "an anti-Jewish archive" of hoaxes and fictions. They reduced the complexity of the world to one single racist explanation that sharply defined the self and other in a single stroke but could be constantly reformulated in different contexts.[9]

In Argentina, one specific issue separated Filippo's anti-Semitic imagination from the European stereotypes that influenced him: his stereotype was linked to a particular imagined history of Jews in Argentina. Along with other fascist groups such as the Argentine Anti-Jewish Action (Acción Antijudía Argentina), he posited a dubious chronicle of Jewish invasions, a fake genealogy of Jewish "infiltration" dating to colonial times.[10] Yet Filippo traced the genealogy of Argentine anti-Semitism not to the colonial era but to Domingo Faustino Sarmiento. Since Sarmiento was, and still is, considered the father of Argentine liberalism and a key architect of the modern state, such a connection, made by an antiliberal such as Filippo, seems bewildering. Filippo hijacked Sarmiento's legacy to give a veneer of legitimacy to his anti-Semitism. Sarmiento was hardly a virulent anti-Semite, but this mattered little to Filippo, who twisted the famous nineteenth-century president's thought to exploit his popularity.[11]

Fascists had no qualms about inventing new roles for old and new friends to help them turn lies into grander truths.[12] Racist lies had direct aims and motivations: discrimination, exclusion, and finally elimination. Anti-Semitic lies had clear consequences that everybody could foresee.[13] Notably, while fascists' explanations for their actions were based on lies, they did not lie about their promises of extermination. They meant what they said. As the Argentine fascists maintained, the Jews were the enemies of the people. Their destiny had to be total elimination: "What a great homage the extermination of these squids would be for our Homeland!"[14]

As Adorno explained in 1945, this extreme dimension of fascism led to torture, persecution, and extermination, and yet almost no one outside the fascists actually took them at their word. Almost nobody considered the true effects of fascist lies and promises of destruction. "The implausibility of their actions," Adorno wrote, "made it easy to disbelieve what nobody, for the sake of precious peace, wanted to believe, while at the same time capitulating to it." The political effects of fascist lies were cemented by unconscious leanings that rendered the untruthful the reality. "Every horror necessarily becomes, in the enlightened world, a horrific fairy-tale," Adorno wrote. "For the untruth of truth has a core which finds an avid response in the unconscious. It is not only that the unconscious wishes horrors to come about; Fascism is itself less 'ideological', in so far as it openly proclaims the principle of domination that is elsewhere concealed."[15]

Fascist racism and anti-Semitism were the consequences of the continuous search for an enemy that defied eternal truths. As they pretended that these truths emanated from the self, fascists needed to create enemies and define them as living embodiments of untruth. These enemies constituted counter-incarnations that helped elevate the leader as the owner of the truth.

The Jews belonged to a long list of enemies of fascism. If in Germany fascists were obsessed with Jews as their main enemies, in the Andes, the Peruvian Blackshirts aimed their animosity against Asian, and especially Japanese, immigrants. In what eventually would become India and Pakistan, fascism adopted Hindu or Muslim undertones. In Argentina, fascists developed "Christianized fascism" as the ultimate proof of the sacred truth of their movement. Mussolini and the Argentine, Japanese, Brazilian, Colombian, Peruvian, and Romanian fascists considered their enemies defining characteristics of their selves. Jews and other enemies were what the fascists were not, and defined, by contrast, what they actually were.

The violence of fascism, and the belief in an absolute truth that motivated it, was a fundamental trigger of the Final Solution but has also appeared in other histories of genocidal violence. As the historian Enzo Traverso argues, the Holocaust was part of a world of converging genocidal ideologies: "The brute violence of the SS special units (Einsatzgruppen) was not a feature peculiar to National Socialism. Rather, it was an indication of how much National Socialism had in common with plenty of the other lethal ideologies of the terrible twentieth century."[16]

Nazism was not an exception but the most radical outcome of the core of fascism: the imbrication of violence, myth, and the fantasy of an eternal truth. For Mussolini, violence and war were sources of political orientation and personal and collective redemption. In these events Mussolini saw the truth of his own violent desires. Spanish fascists talked of the "sacred violence of action," which was equally rooted in justice and right. The motto of the Egyptian Blue Shirts was "Obedience and Struggle" (al-ṭā'a wa al-jihād), and this idea was also reflected in their oath: " I swear by almighty God, by my honour and by the fatherland that I will be a faithful and obedient soldier, fighting for the sake of Egypt, and that I will abstain from whatever would pervert my principles or be harmful to my organization." A world away from the Middle East, the Chinese Blue Shirts asserted that violence had to be directed toward all political rivals: "There must be a determination to shed blood—that is, there must be a kind of unprecedented violence to eliminate all enemies of the people."

According to the Colombian fascists, the Leopards, "Violence, as illuminated by the myth of a beautiful and heroic fatherland, [was the only thing that could] create for us a favorable alternative in the great fights of the future." Fascists connected violence and death to a radical renewal of the self. For them, it was a means of revelation of the true will of men. For example, the Romanian fascists linked the sacred nature of violence to the idea of the sacrificial death, regeneration, and salvation of their warriors. For them, as "God wanted" it, "the germ of a renewal can grow only out of death, of suffering." As a result, Romanian fascists "love[d] death." Death was "our dearest wedding among weddings."[17]

Fascists worldwide shared a notion of truth that rested in the sacred. This truth, which did not need empirical corroboration and overlapped with an idea of godly justice, made legality a moot issue. For Chilean fascists, violence could not be stopped by "juridical formalities" and it was "licit" as a preemptive response to left-wing violence.[18] For the Romanians, belief in anti-Semitic fantasy resulted in a fight that transcended almost every norm. After the "recognition that Jewish domination is leading us to spiritual and national death," few doubts remained that "death to the traitor" was the only possible path.[19] There were no juridical mechanisms that could stand between the fascists and the need to destroy their enemies, and this idea of summary justice rested on the notion of eternal truth. Fascism's messianic religious conception relied on creating an enemy that, as they imagined it, stood against the truth and thereby needed to be repressed and eventually eliminated.

5   Truth and Power

"Mussolini is always right."[1] Between 1922 and 1945, Italian fascists repeated this impossible sentence like liturgy. They believed that Mussolini owned the truth.[2] But what kind of truth? How could truth encompass the past and the present and then project itself into the future? Fascists' answers to this question made explicit fascism's own reliance on a continuum that transcended the historical and the empirical. As critical thinkers like Freud and Borges suggested at the time, this was the key mythical dimension of fascism.[3] In a work that, according to Adorno, "foresaw" the rise and nature of fascism, Freud observed that the myth of the hero was at the center of group psychology and the imaginative displacement of reality that Adorno would later apply to his own analysis of fascism. Freud wrote, "The lie of the heroic myth culminates in the deification of the hero."[4]

In 1933, in an act of profound ironic density, Freud signed a copy of one of his books for Mussolini, calling him a hero. The Duce missed the implication, as many current historians still do. In fact, Freud was deeply critical of hero worship, because he saw it in the context of contemporary mass politics. For him, modern "heroes" served and promoted people's needs for vertical authority. Freud was concerned by what he saw as the return of the authoritarian primal father in the form of modern political myths. These modern heroes demanded full submission to their aggressive desires, ending in total domination.[5]

As Arendt noted, the first pledge for members of the Nazi party included the statement, "The Führer is always right." Hitler himself said that "infallibility" marked the superiority of his movement.[6] In fact, many fascists believed that Mussolini's or Hitler's infallibility was real precisely because it was mythical. The leader was constructed as representing a continuity with Greek and Roman peoples and heroes. Like them, the dictator represented the thinking of the nation, "its time and space." Fascism launched a new era. The leader was supposed to have a unique epochal genius.[7]

In fascism, belief was intimately linked to an act of faith in the conductor. Fascism presented its leaders as living myths. While in Germany the *Führerprinzip* featured Hitler as the ultimate source of truth and authority, in Argentina, Spain, and beyond, fascists identified the politics of their leaders with a transcendental mythical truth. The truth of fascism connected the reality of the movement and its leaders with a mythical past of heroism, violence, and subordination. In fascist ideology, the leaders personified a direct link with this epochal continuum, establishing a unitary front with the people and the nation. In turn, the dictator was the definitive source of popular sovereignty, responsible only to himself. As Hitler argued, "He who personifies Germany's highest peak receives his calling from the German *Volk* and is obligated to it alone!"[8]

Fascists were obsessed with the infallibility of their leaders because, for them, the lack of error reflected the core divine truths of the mythical ideology that had incarnated in the heroic conductor of men. The Spanish fascist Ernesto Giménez Caballero made this principle of mythical embodiment a major element in his "general theory of fascism." Finding theoretical roots in Carlyle's idea of history but more important in Nietzsche's "new Titan" and Sorel's idea of revolutionary violence, Giménez Caballero argued that Mussolini and Hitler were the leaders who best embodied the new concept of the hero in "the current history of the world." Mussolini was not like previous heroes, and yet many heroes had something of Mussolini in them. He was like Achilles, Caesar, Charlemagne, and Charles V—but all these were incomplete when compared with the Duce. Even "Napoleon was a failed Mussolini." Giménez Caballero asserted that Mussolini's heroic nature was "unlike the Greek, Eastern, Christian, Renaissance and Romantic type of heroism." He embodied and surpassed the sum of all previous heroes as a new living myth: "Today no one doubts—no one should doubt—that Mussolini has incarnated a new and current Heroicity in history."[9]

Unlike liberalism and socialism, which they considered were based in nontranscendental roots, on partial truths or even lies, fascists longed for a return of the mythical warring heroes. This is what they expected from their leaders. As Lugones warmly said to the Argentine dictator General José F. Uriburu, "Don't listen to the university intellectuals [doctores], my general. It is enough with your consciousness of patriot and soldier. General Uriburu is always right when he thinks like General Uriburu."[10] Similarly, the Spanish fascist General José Millán Astray asserted that as a soldier, Franco "is never wrong."[11]

Leaders embodied a faith, a belief in a truth that had to be accepted without discussing it. What was at stake was the future of the world. In 1935, a legionnaire had to adhere to the "ten commandments" of the Romanian fascist legion "in order not to deviate from his glorious path in these days of darkness, of misfortune and satanic temptation. Then, everyone knows that we are legionnaires and we will remain legionnaires for eternity." The first commandment dealt with the key issue of what *not* to believe in: "Do not believe in any way in the information, in the news about the legionary movement read in any newspaper—even if it seems nationalist—or whispered by agents or even by honest people. The legionnaire believes only in the orders and in the word of his leader."[12]

While for antifascists like Arendt fascists simply ignored the truth, for the fascists themselves, truth transcended the sensory or empirical world. As ideal embodiments of national authenticity, leaders represented the authentic truth. However, as Jacques Derrida cogently argued at his University of Buenos Aires lecture on the conceptual history of lying, Arendt did not sufficiently consider the dynamic interplay between the unconscious and the status of truth in the act of political lying. Derrida stresses the need to pay more attention to the logic of the unconscious and to what he sees as a theory of performativity in the act of lying. Arendt, meanwhile, suggested but did not develop the phantasmatic aspects of lying, what Derrida defines as the spectral dimensions of the unconscious.[13] This totalitarian return to the unconscious was rooted in the longing for a mythical absence, a founding national trauma. Truth was related to the disclosure of this absence as the acting out of imagined and real collective traumas.[14]

The return of the sacred past, so often invoked in totalitarian texts (the thousand-year Reich, Augustan imperial Rome, Pharaonic Egypt, Imperial China, or the Viceroyalty of Rio de la Plata in Argentina), signaled the fascist attempt to revoke ongoing processes of secularization. Rather than believe that they were, as the German philosopher Hans Blumenberg would have it, reoccupying spaces previously occupied by religion, fascists actually believed that they were performing a true religion. They agreed in practice with Martin Heidegger that the sacred actually referred to the trace of "the gods that have left" and that leads back to their return.[15] This was the messianic aspect of fascism. Whereas in Nazism this trace was actualized in the conception and practice of redemptive anti-Semitism, in most fascisms it tended to be more diffusely located in political violence, war, imperialism, and racism.[16]

To understand the role of truth in fascism it is important to consider how and why fascist theory established a radical boundary between reason and unreason, with violence at the center of this divide. Fascists considered that the emergence of inner authenticity became a meaningful political act when it implied redemption through violence, sacrifice, and death.

The revolution against the revolution was a result of self-persuasion regarding the relationship between truth and power (embodied in the leader) that would lead to salvation. The Spanish fascist Ramiro de Maeztu argued, "For a long time, I have had the persuasion that this whole period of confusion and vacillations will end up generating an overwhelming counterrevolutionary movement. It will engender the salvation of Spain."[17] As the Spanish fascists claimed at the start of their civil war (and after the death of de Maeztu at the hands of antifascists), "Force, blood and martyrdom are at the service of the Truth."[18] In the same context, the Chinese fascists argued that since morality had been abused only power could represent the truth: "Truth has been entirely violated by force. Therefore, unless there is force, there can be no truth."[19] Here, as elsewhere in fascism, truth emerged from the self by way of the individual's submission to the cause. This totalitarian view of truth did not consider it universal. Its criterion was ideological.

This truth was based in faith. It was rooted in the self's discovery of eternal knowledge hidden in myth.

The Nazi Alfred Rosenberg, the most racist theorist of myth, maintained, "Today a new faith is awakening—the Mythos of the blood; the belief that to defend the blood is also to defend the divine nature of man in general. It is a belief, effulgent with the brightest knowledge, that Nordic blood represents that *Mysterium* which has overcome and replaced the older sacraments." The revelation of this mystery could only be accomplished through "a review of history"—a reading of the past deformed by anti-Semitic lies. But for Rosenberg, it was a path that equally combined a renaissance of consciousness and the destruction of the Other: "To become fully conscious" of the myth "is to create the basis for every rebirth. It is the foundation of a new world view, of a new-yet-old idea of the State, of the mythos of a new comprehension of life, which alone will give us the strength to throw off the arrogant dominion of the subhumans, and to construct a culture in conformity with our own racial character, permeating all facets of existence."[20]

Fascists regarded any theory as true only when it was attached to the sacred, which in countries like Argentina, Italy, Brazil, and Spain they associated with classical or Christian myths, while in Germany it was centrally related to a legend of the Aryan race. The myth of blood and soil was taken to grotesque extreme by the Romanian Legion's "death squads [who] ritually drank each other's blood."[21] The esoteric racism of Julius Evola's "Myth of the Blood" was thus perhaps most fitting in the German or Romanian cases rather than in the Italian one.[22]

The fantasy of the blood myth became a form of legitimation encompassing national lands, morality, and justice. It was not only in Germany that justice was an essential part of the leader's representation and creation of the truth. But in Germany, the truth of the leader was judicially constructed to the full extent as a replacement for more rational forms of law. Juridical truth was equated with the transcendental nature of the leader. Hitler famously represented himself as "the supreme judge of the Nation."[23] To be sure, it is highly probable that Carl Schmitt was insincere when, in 1934, he claimed that the Fuhrer was the embodiment of the "most authentic jurisdiction." But Schmitt, a latecomer to Nazism who had a perceptive and sympathetic take on its mythical connotations, fully understood the Nazi notion of truth when he stated that Hitler was "not subjected to justice" but rather constituted the highest form of justice.

For the Nazis, Hitler was the ultimate source of justice precisely because, as Schmitt argued, the judiciary nature of the Fuhrer emanated from the same vital source as the right of the people (*Volksrecht*).[24] In Nazi Germany, Hitler was the leader, the supreme judge, and, as Nazi Minister of Justice Hans Frank affirmed, the only legislator. According to the antifascist thinker Antonio Gramsci, the Nazis radically questioned the notion of an abstract universal justice. Gramsci argued that their notion of the law had become an "article of faith" for adherents.[25] For Frank himself, justice existed only when it followed the needs of the *Volk* as interpreted by Hitler. The will of Hitler, the fascist sense of truth in his sacred leadership, was formulated as German public law.

The Nazis therefore gave juridical status to the more extended fascist revolutionary conception that the leader determined the truthfulness of his own actions and desires. As the full embodiment of the people and the national self, the fascist dictator was the recipient and also the creator of right. He was the imagined source of what Hans Frank called "the categorical imperative of the Third

Reich[:] ... Act in such a way that the Führer, if he knew your action, would approve it." As Arendt pointed out, Eichmann might have been aware of this imperative, which was analogous to his "unconscious distortion" of the Kantian formula. Arendt suggested that Eichmann perceived what he later (in Jerusalem) called "crimes legalized by the state" as having a legal basis because they emanated from Hitler's will. In short, for the Nazis, the leader became the law because he represented ideological truth; his "words had the force of law."[26]

With his words, the leader created the conditions for representing and determining the truth. Brazilian fascists understood the voice of the fascist leader Plínio Salgado to have created both the Integralista movement and the idea behind it, the new "integralist gospel."[27] Salgado represented his own sacred leadership as the continuation of classical European myths and modern Latin America ones. His "Bolivarian politics" hoped to articulate an international sense of "sentimental, cultural, and economic unity" in a Latin America moving in an *integralista* direction. "We are living the century, par excellence, of South America," Salgado wrote. "The century of 'intuition.' After a century of experimentation, which has become as dogmatic as all the apriorisms it has fought against, we come to the threshold of an Age which, without abandoning deductive methods, at the same time serves inductive methods."[28]

Similarly, for the fascist Silvio Villegas, of the Colombian Leopards, Bolívar was the hero and theorist of antidemocratic possibilities. Villegas argued that "bolivarismo is the only immortal aspect" of the Latin American spirit. For him, "only Truth is the means to assess ideas." Citing Lugones, the Leopards identified political decadence with ugliness and equality. Like Lugones, the

Colombians equated their own politics with a notion of beauty that transcended time, with a foundation in the "spiritual legacy" of ancient Greece and the Roman Empire.[29] For Salgado, too, Latin American unity represented not a pragmatic aim but a desire for a "synthesis" that emanated from the inner self, and which had been previously incarnated by Bolívar. Latin America was "a whole subconscious world that has remained dormant under the political and literary exteriorities with which we have been deluded for more than a century."[30]

Salgado was not the only leader unveiling and personifying these deep Latin American undercurrents. Lugones also proposed "a true natural confederation" of South American countries, with a central role for Argentina. Unlike Salgado's myth of Atlantis and his theory of Bolivarian incarnation, Lugones rejected any Latin American differentiation from Europe. For him, the best way of being Latin American was to be "white." Before the rise of Uriburu, Lugones also saw in Mussolini a mythical figure who had impersonated the "return to Rome." He argued that the "hour of the sword," Lugones's famous call for the dawn of dictatorship in Latin America, was the time for primordial forms of domination, for the organic integration of truth and power. After the coup of 1930, the voice and the word of the dictator General Uriburu were ritually conceived as a unitary program representing the promise of collective redemption. As Lugones pointed out, the persona of Uriburu synthesized the "people and the army." At a time when the enemies of the people refuted national consciousness, the dictator personified it and then revealed it to the nation. This is why for fascists the leader owned the truth.

6 Revelations

Italian fascists stressed that Mussolini had revealed to them "Eternal truths."[1] For them, Mussolini's words expressed the reality of the age. Fascists believed that the Duce's words allowed them to understand "the spirit of man." His words represented reality from the towering gaze of an "inflexible will."[2] But this was not only a question of perspective. His voice was absolute. It was supposed to stand for all forms of representation, including artistic ones.[3]

Mussolini was the source of a new fascist world. He was "the one without an equal." Fascist songs insisted on Mussolini's uniqueness and transcendental meaning-making. They imagined that his "Word" was the source of mobilization. He even illuminated the dead. The path of "destiny" was in his hands. As the fascist song "The Legionary Eagle" proclaimed, Mussolini embodied "genius, faith, passion, and truth."[4]

Italian fascists were confronted with the "tremendous task of creating the analytic corpus of fascist civilization by commenting on the thinking of Mussolini." As the fascist Federico Forni put it in 1939, fascism was both the "creation and the representation of the world." Thus, truth was not only observed but also actively constructed. In other words, truth was the result of a "revolution in the making [*revoluzione in atto*]." If "knowledge" from the eighteenth century to the early twentieth century had been "scientific," fascism had effectively changed the course of the history of political perception, abandoning the notion of scientific falsifiability because "fascism is immutable and eternal in its fundamental principles." As opposed to the malleable scientific notion of truth, Forni argued, "as a mythical movement that regards its reality not as a demonstration but as a faith, fascism is a-scientific. As a believed truth it overcomes the demonstrated truth."[5]

Similarly, Alfred Rosenberg maintained that "the logical part of this entire truth is the manipulation of the tools of understanding and reason, as represented by the critique of perception. The intuitive part of the whole truth is revealed in art, fairy tales, and religious mythos." For Rosenberg, what was perceived could only be accepted if it was in "the service of organic truth." In practice, this meant standing in the service of the racial myth. Perceptions could transition to an acceptable form of truth if they enhanced the "shape and inner values of this race-Volkhood" and cultivated it "more purposefully and shape[d] it more vitally." As a result of what he saw as the integration of mythical intuition and perception, "the primordial conflict between knowing and believing, if not resolved, is taken back to its organic foundation and a new observation is rendered possible." Rosenberg stated that it was "fundamentally" perverse that in mythless notions of truth "the search for the one 'absolute eternal truth' was grasped purely as an affair of knowing, i.e., as an affair of something which was, if not technically, then approximately, attainable." This was wrong, he said, because "the last possible will of a race is already contained in its first religious mythos. The recognition of this fact is the last actual wisdom of man."[6]

Even when fascists believed that myths and empirical observation could be organically merged, they denied that truth, by its nature sacred, could be independently derived from empirical observation. Revelation was, instead, an outcome of political mythical inquiries into the soul of the *ethnōs*. As Salgado, the Brazilian fascist leader, saw it, the nation was "bringing from the bottom of autochthonous energies the mysterious poem that reveals itself in the unity of the wild Theogony and even in the identity of the vocabulary roots of languages also in the nascent state." Latin America was a "Solar continent, which brings to the breast the line of the Equator, like a strange necklace of light, and on the head the Tropic of Cancer as a diadem, and to the womb the luminous belt of the Tropic of Capricorn, in the recess of the soul it guards, ignored to itself, the worship of the Inca veils by the Sun."[7]

Likewise, for Rosenberg, the racial "instinctual" submission of the people to the leader represented a new era of the spirit. It was "the triumph of the spirit over the brute force of matter." In the world of fascism, Mussolini's trinity "believe, obey, fight" implied the realization of justice. As the Great Council of Fascism stated in 1935 with respect to the imperial fascist war on Ethiopia, we "enthusiastically acclaim the Duce as the realizer of the supreme right of the nation."[8]

In fascism, the leader's ideology defined the truth. The antifascist Alexandre Koyré interpreted this phenomenon in 1943: "The official philosophies of the totalitarian regimes unanimously brand as nonsensical the idea that there exists a single objective truth valid for everybody." Koyré called this phenomenon a radical activist understanding of the truth. Totalitarian theorists therefore denied the innate value of thought: "for them, thought is not a light but a weapon; its function, they say, is not to discover reality as it is but to change and transform it with the purpose of leading us toward what is not." For Koyré, myth and affect disastrously replaced empirical forms of verification: "Such being the case, myth is better than science and rhetoric that works on the *passions* preferable to proof that appeals to the intellect."⁹

Fascists and antifascists shared categories and even vocabularies but sharply differed on their political meanings and legitimacy. Thus, on the other side of the political spectrum, the Argentine fascist poet Leopoldo Lugones argued that "demonstrable truth" did not reveal the ultimate truth. The latter he equated with heroism, nationalism, and beauty. If liberalism had a phenomenological sense of truth, this was a half-truth. For Lugones, fascism represented a truth that was both in and outside of history. Its roots were in the Greco-Latin classical world, Christianity, and the Spanish conquest of America, and it represented a patriotic rebellion against liberalism. But it also was a transhistorical sacred trend. In Lugones's version of Argentine clerico-fascism, truth was equally an aspect of power and the divine.¹⁰

Like Lugones, de Maeztu posited the existence of an "eternal truth." It was in the search for right and truth "as transcendental essences" that reality emerged.¹¹ Similarly, Gustavo Barroso, the most important fascist intellectual of Brazil, argued that Brazilian fascism was the best political formation on earth because it represented "eternal truths." These promised a transcendental change, the "new times" when the "unity" of the spirit, the cross, and the nation would rule.¹² Like Lugones and de Maeztu, Barroso identified the rise of a new era with the aesthetic and political primacy of absolute truth.¹³ The leader of the Brazilian fascist integralistas, Salgado, was more explicit. Historical times were replaced with mythical times: "Today Latin America is the great region of the world because of a fatality that finds its explanation at the dawn of time." The "disappearance of Atlantis" had a clear relationship to the Latin American present. It was the epic moment that signaled "the dawn of a civilization that will have nothing in common with all the others."[14] Understanding fatality through mythical introspection would lead to the truth about the past and the present.

Fascism was the revelation of a new world: "The work of Brazilian Integralism today represents the fatality of that feeling, of the instincts of the earth, the revelation of the muted voices of the human mass of the Continent." Brazil and Latin America were the *ultima thule*, a mythically distant unknown region at the end of the world. "We are the Last West," Salgado claimed. "And because we are the Last West, we are the First East [Primeiro Oriente]. We are a New World. We are the Fourth Humanity. We are the Aurora of the Future Times. We are the force of the Earth. We are again what were, in the remotest of ages, those who wrote in the heavenly history of their march that began in the luminous gate of Aries by the zodiacal script."[15]

The reality of the present, the true form of the "explanation," was that of revelation. Lugones, de Maeztu, Barroso, and Salgado were not alone among transatlantic fascists in representing truth as the fusion of a mythical version of history, the idea of politics as the vehicle for the sacred, the equation of beauty and right politics, and the notion that justice was fully subordinated to power. In fascism, truth was considered real because it was rooted in emotional emanations of the soul, images and actions that fascists identified with political ideology. Action, soul searching, and faith displaced programmatic considerations.

As the Romanian fascist Corneliu Codreanu warned, developing a complete and explicit program was against the interests of the

fascist movement. Faith, and a renewal of souls, was more important than a program. Romanian fascists "have a doctrine," he
wrote, "they have a religion. This is something of higher order that
mysteriously unites thousands of men determined to forge another
destiny. While men serve their program or doctrine with some
interest, the legionaries are men of great faith and at any moment
they are ready to sacrifice themselves for this faith. They deeply
serve this faith." Codreanu concluded that faith was better than a
program, because while nobody would die for a program, fascists
were willing to die for their faith. Fascism was a "great spiritual
school." It created a devotion that would be a "revolution of the
soul." The main political aim of Romanian fascism was to change
the "soul of the individual and the soul of the people." This was a
politics of truth that stood against the enemy's lies, or as Codreanu
put it, a matter of fighting the corruption of the self that the enemy
promoted. "The new programs and the social systems lavishly
flaunted before the people are a lie if an evil soul hides in their
shadow." Lies were not empirically falsifiable statements; for
Codreanu, rather, they were the expression of a "lack of consciousness towards the fulfillment of duty, the same spirit of betrayal to
everything that is Romanian."[16]

Action was needed against these lies. As the British fascist
leader Sir Oswald Mosley argued, fascist action was antithetical to
democratic dialogue. Action was at the center of "the true patriotism of fascism."[17] Conversely, while both Arendt and Koyré saw
fascism as simply opposed to truth, more interestingly, both also
noted the centrality of images in the fascist understanding of
truth.[18] As I have argued elsewhere, Sigmund Freud and Jorge Luis
Borges, two very different contemporary authors, both addressed
this particular dimension. For Borges, as he wrote in the journal

Nosotros in 1925, fascism and "Lugoneria" (that is, the fascism of Lugones made famous through his proclamation of the "hour of the sword") implied an "exaltation" of the senses that did not help thought. Borges equated fascism with "intellectual slippery slopes [tropezones intelectuales]." For Freud, fascism inhabited a world of fantasy where myths and leaders ruled over the reality principle.[19] For both, the problem of fascism was that it applied a lie— and a violent, barbaric ideology—to the structural truth of the classical mythical world. It represented not only the return of the repressed gods, their homecoming to the world overcome by reason, but also their totalitarian political adoption.

For Borges and Freud alike, fascism's lack of truth was related to its unreason, its unwarrented transformation of old plural myths into unitary political mythology. Freud conceptualized fascism as a pathological take on truth. For Borges, Nazi anti-Semitism was rooted in a "learned hallucination." For both, fascism represented the denial of contextual truths (that is, history). Both stressed the relationship in fascism between violence, racism, and faith. For Borges, fascism was utterly destructive; men could only lie, kill, and spill blood for Nazism, which was incapable of promoting any positive outcome. Fascist violence was "the faith of the sword," a transcendental form rooted in an "ethics of infamy." Borges signaled this ideological dimension in a comment he made during World War II: that Germans had to be indoctrinated, taking "seminars of abnegation" in this ethics of violence. But Nazi ethics was a contradiction in terms, a "non-ethics [*la ninguna ética del nazismo*]."

This was not a rational ethical education that emanated from books; it was drawn, rather, from images and emotions. It was, in short, the return of superstition. As such, Borges identified fascism as antithetical to reading. In 1944, he warned that fascism would eventually lead to the destruction of knowledge. It would open the way to the "death of all books on earth." Ironically, since he did not have Borges's 1944 knowledge of the then-ongoing extermination of the Jews, Freud also ironically argued that book burning was better than body burning. For Freud, the Nazi burning of his books represented the fascist rejection of learned culture: "What progress we are making. In the Middle Ages they would have burnt me; nowadays they are content with burning my books."[20]

In this context, the epistemological excesses of some fascists did go so far as to deny the value of reading as a source of political knowledge.[21] But for most fascists, thought needed to be fused with action. As Mussolini put it, the book and the musket make the perfect fascist: "Libro e moschetto, fascista perfetto."[22] Fascists had a very ambivalent relation to books and culture. To be sure, fascism was underpinned by strong intellectual currents, including futurism and other forms of the modern in literature and the arts. But fascism also embraced anti-intellectualism as a key source of political motivation. As the Peruvian Marxist intellectual José Carlos Mariátegui argued, for the authentic fascist, fascism "is not a concept." Fascism opposed art in the name of violence. Mussolini's ideological stances were "motorized by sentiment."

Mariátegui had analyzed basic dimensions of fascism in the 1920s, especially its constitutive anti-Enlightenment dimensions. The movement was against "freedom and democracy but also against grammar."[23] It made the ideological decision to reject culture. Similarly, for Adorno, fascist sentimentalism did not imply a simple "primitive, unreflecting emotion" but rather a clear decision to simulate or imitate what was supposed to be the world of the unconscious. Fascists consciously sought this "collective retrogression." Fascism offered its followers a fiction of real feelings and not a simple form of irrationalism.[24]

For fascists, abstractions and problematic symbolism potentially and fatally implied liberalism and democracy. The textual was potentially dangerous for the fascist plan to return to the world of emotions and images. The text as a necessary conceptualization was dangerously distanced from a sensorial state. Concepts and principles were regarded as mirages of reason that fascism needed to correct. Ironically, for fascists, "consciousness" was the result of a violent externalization of truth, moving from violent performative acts that subverted the symbolic and analogical order of things to actual, explicit violence and conquest. Consciousness and instincts were mutually organic to the fascist totalitarian state.[25] In short, the quest to unearth the mythical forces of the unconscious defined the fascist idea of consciousness.

7   The Fascist Unconscious

Fascism supposedly represented a collective vehicle for the expression and political tuning of an authentic being. This idea that the soul had an authentic inner notion of the world was at the center of the fascist intellectual process. It was at the root of fascists' understanding of the political. Mussolini's brother Arnaldo, for example, argued that the will dominating fascism promoted an internal and general renewal. He actually argued that Mussolini's job was to tune this collective anima. Politics, more than art, could grasp and transform the soul and project it into the future. In short, fascism understood the soul as the source of its political legitimacy.[1]

The individual and collective desires of the people were embodied in the persona of the leader. The leader was, in a sense, the expression of fascist ideas of sovereignty. To be sure, this sovereignty was rooted in the collective will—but only nominally. Only the leader was the ideal representation of sovereign desires. He fully understood the collective aspirations of the nation, or, to put it differently, he knew better than the people what they truly wanted. As Hitler saw it, the role of the leader was to fulfill the desires of the people because "the common people themselves harbor indefinite desires and have general convictions, but cannot obtain precise clarity regarding the actual nature of their aim or of their own desire, let alone the possibility of its fulfillment."[2]

The role of the conductor, the "strongest man," was derived from the "natural order." Hitler's language suggested that the people's inner conviction that the leader was the one and only person who truly mattered was akin to a form of religious renewal. Before a leader could act publicly, he would have to emerge out of a popular "psychic urge." For Hitler, nations that could not find a "heroic solution" were "impotent." The opposite of this state was the fulfillment of political desires through the incarnation of the entire people in the persona of the leader: "Fate some day bestows upon it the man endowed for this purpose, who finally brings the long yearned-for fulfillment." Hitler saw the advent of such a man as the outcome of a mythical struggle, a transhistorical destiny that could not be factually corroborated. The conductor was "the best man" set by history in "the place where he belonged. This will always be so and will eternally remain so, as it always has been so." In this mythical vision of linear connections between the past and the present, Hitler opposed "truth" to "so-called human wisdom." History involved conscious and "unconscious struggles for hegemony."[3]

Mussolini also saw himself as the primary interpreter of an unconscious collective. The French strand of reactionary protofascist thought put forward a similar vision. Maurice Barrès exalted the "primacy of the unconscious," and Charles Maurras insisted that instincts and the unconscious were central to the organization of a society.[4] The legitimacy of fascism was based on this unique notion that political legitimacy was derived from the unconscious. According to this definition, popular sovereignty could not be the electoral expression of a popular majority but its dual dictatorial actualization in the fascist state and its leader. Fascism was incarnated in the totalitarian state that Mussolini created. As the Italian fascist Michele Bianchi argued, "The personality of the state is alive and it is not an abstract concept or a juridical formula. But it is a sentiment and a will: the sentiment and the will of the nation." Thus, Bianchi made the case that the state under Mussolini was not only a political reality but also "an ideal and ethical reality."[5]

This "will of the nation" was a result of the state's conquest by fascism. It was not a generic state but the fascist state. It was rooted in the fascist perception, and acting out, of the mythical unconscious. The fascist dictatorship became its externalization. This notion of the unconscious was ideological in the sense that proponents expected it to transcend a more factual level of perception. But these claims about the inner authenticity of fascist politics were, in fact, a fascist rationalization. In other words, they constituted a rationale for the fascist political and nonprogrammatic emphasis on drives, myths, and fantasies. Thus, ironically, the fascist unconscious was necessarily the result of a conscious act.

According to the fascist view, the people's power was permanently delegated to the leader, who acted as the best expression of the people's ideal self. The leader embodied the sovereignty of the people. If monarchs had embodied themselves, the fascist leader's claim to legitimacy rested in the people. But in fascist rhetoric and belief this legitimacy was not devoid of divine connotations. For Mussolini, the "sovereignty of the people" existed only through absolute delegation of power to the leader, who ruled by force, not consensus.[6] But Mussolini's interpretation was exemplified not only in his readings of the existing popular will or the confirmation of the "people certainty of their potency" but also, more important, in his own intuitions. Like Hitler, the Duce thought that he knew what the people really wanted. He imagined he could feel the "pulse of the nation" from within.[7]

As a result, even when fascists expressed an admiration for the French theorist Georges Sorel, they were critical of his instrumental take. Sorel believed in the political power of myths without having faith in them. For Salgado, the Brazilian fascists' leader, Sorel's problem was his reduction of history to class struggle; "the technique of Sorel" was therefore opposed to "the technique of Christ." In short, Sorel lacked belief. He was "genial and insufficient." As the Colombian fascists noted, Sorellian theory could produce communism as well its "antidotes": fascism and Nazism. They argued that "violence is the only maker, but this is not possible without creating an epic state of the soul." These states could be produced by "religion, glory, or a great political myth." Mussolini himself stated that "Sorel is truly *nôtre maître*." But while the Duce presented Sorel as one of the authors who contributed to the formation of his "mentality," he also expressed a significant disagreement regarding morality. All in all, Mussolini's belief in the reality of the mythical went far beyond Sorellian instrumental views of myth.[8]

Mussolini conflated the desires of the people (as deduced by himself) with those of the sacred. In 1926, he stated that when thinking about the historical destiny of the nation, he was able to "see" the work of a sacrosanct will, "the infallible hand of providence, the infallible sign of divinity" in the unfolding of events.[9] Many fascists concurred. For them, Mussolini's mind demonstrated the "sublime permeation of the divine in the human." Mussolini's soul was considered the collective embodiment of all souls, the ideal source for reading inner Italian authenticity.[10] The result was Mussolini's ability to constantly reformulate fascism through the relentless defense of whatever he did or said, that is to say, the political realizations of his fantasies and desires. As the fascist intellectual Camillo Pellizzi put it, there was no need for fascist dogma insofar as this dogma was primarily represented by Mussolini's persona and actions.[11] As if displaying a theory of political drives, this totalizing of Mussolini's agency was often explained as the result of an affirmation of life over death, as in the anthem to the "heroes of the fascist revolution." Mussolini himself equated life with a radical sense of struggle.[12]

For fascists, instincts, soul, character, and personality were mythical embodiments, biological realities as well as collective legacies of the imperial past. Devoid of rational mediations, fascist inner selves were no longer mental abstractions but living representations of the imperial myth of the nation. As opposed to the abstract distinction between the body and the mind, Pellizzi argued that the "soul" was an "absorbent reality [*realtà assorbente*]."[13] Fascists conceived their politics as expressing this "reality" through the "immanent" experiences of violence, war, and imperialism. Empire was an essential expression of the "hierarchical instinct."[14] All in all, the fascist idea of the unconscious emphasized the necessity of recognizing the leader's needs as a true emanation of destructive drives— that is, an affirmation of violent desires. In short, fascism believed itself to embody pure desire but at the same time repressed all desire unrelated to the main points of ideological fascism: total war, full-fledged violence, and the destruction of the enemy.[15] Fascism represented the absolutization of violent drives in the political sphere. This was encapsulated by the Mussolinean idea of "living dangerously" or, as the Spanish fascist Giménez Caballero put it, a creative danger infused with mysticism. Giménez Caballero's perfect fascist world was one where the notions of "pain and war" had an "affirmative and supernatural value."[16]

The idea that a subject would find transcendental value "in pain and war" is a testament to the dehumanizing dimensions of the fascist idea that truth belongs to the world of the supernatural rather than to human history and agency. This belief in a sacred form of truth had clear Christian theological connotations. In the Bible, the Lord's truth contrasts with the lies of men: "Although everyone is a liar, let God be proved true." Those who do not believe the truth of God are literally demonized: "Who is the liar but the one who denies that Jesus is the Christ? This is the antichrist, the one who denies the Father and the Son." The lies of the unfaithful emanated from the devil. They wanted to judge according to human standards and stood against the truthful understanding that only faith could provide: "Why do you not understand what I say? It is because you cannot accept my word. You are from your father the devil, and you choose to do your father's desires. He was a murderer from the beginning and does not stand in the truth, because there is no truth in him. When he lies, he speaks according to his own nature, for he is a liar and the father of lies."[17] Fascism's idea of truth grew from this traditional set of oppositions between divine truth and demonic lies. As the Argentine fascist priest Leonardo Castellani claimed in 1943, the only way to reach the truth was to "translate" it from God. The result would be the displacement of scientific truth in favor of "mystic truth."[18]

As a result, fascism renounced self-awareness and put in its place a Godly truth supposedly emanating from a purified self. As Giménez Caballero complained, "Man has analyzed his own conscience far too much; he has ended up corroding and diluting it, by not believing in the unity of what cannot be divided. And that is the secret behind the bastardy of Freudianism and superrealism." Freudian theory was part of the culture of the leftist and Jewish enemy. It was both the essence of primitivism and a hallmark of secular modernity: "Both the primitive man of the Paleolithic and the savage of today have been Freudian without knowing it."[19]

Interpreting Freudian theory as a desire to have a transcendental sense of the truth—which was in fact a critical element of his theory of the self—fascists like Giménez Caballero defended a nationalist and religious notion of truth. This truth could be reached by leaving all doubt behind in order to embrace a "faith in the truth of a naked intellect." This path from an individual to a collective state was fascist politics in a nutshell: "The art of life is . . . achieving the passage from an individual state to the state of the fatherland, in order to then reach a supreme eternal state: of peace and the contemplation of God." He asserted, "Let us obey with the individual discipline of a musical note in a melody that only God pulsates in and listens to."[20]

In invoking a truth residing beyond human history, in surrendering critical inquiries into the self, fascist political theology presented a sacred path to reality. This move implied a rejection of perception and an almost complete alienation from reality. It led fascist believers to a profound distrust of the self-awareness derived from psychoanalytic technique. Why was this critique of Freud important to fascists? What was at stake for them in their battles against psychoanalysis? These questions are taken up next.

8 Fascism against Psychoanalysis

As a young poet just returned from Europe, Jorge Luis Borges wrote to a Spanish friend in 1921 about an ambitious—perhaps impossible—literary project, a collective and fantastic novel to be written with Macedonio Fernández and other literary friends. The plot, Borges said, would revolve around a fictional Bolshevik plan to gain power by spreading a "general neurosis" among the Argentine people.[1] Borges, of course, never wrote this novel, and he probably could not have foreseen that anyone would envision the hypothetical plot as an actual threat to the nation. Yet this was exactly the threat that a group of fascists in Argentina identified as a Jewish conspiracy—even pointing to Borges himself as an actor in the plot. According to this group, Jews both epitomized collective neurosis and conspired to gain control of the country by spreading the disease. Freudian psychoanalysis was here both a means and an end.

Fascist ideas about the mystic, violent, and hierarchical self are in sharp contrast to psychoanalytic theory. For many fascists, psychoanalytic categories of the unconscious applied only to the enemy. In turn, by denying the sacred dimension of fascism and presenting it as the return of a Western form of barbarism, Freud opposed not only fascist ends, but fascist self-understanding. For Leopoldo Lugones, Freud symbolized the unacceptable: he questioned the idea of the sacred and therefore the politics that fascism represented. For Freud, Lugones wrote, "God is no more than the idealization, in itself bipolarized, of the *Totem* or beast-pet that some savage tribes possess."[2] He represented an "anti-religion" that emphasized the negativity of instinctual forces. Lugones regarded psychoanalysis as above all "anti-Christian" and thus antithetical to the eternal truth of a Christian fascism.

At the same time, Argentine clerico-fascists like Virgilio Filippo were worried about psychoanalytic perspectives on normality, desire, and pathology. In short, Freudian theories apparently posed a threat to transcendental truths about the self and the sacred. Filippo was one of the most important of Freudianism's anti-Semitic adversaries during this period. Like many fellow Argentine fascists, he saw Freudian psychoanalysis as a threat to the nation. This perception was based on a particular vision of the "internal enemy" and a primarily secularized, racialized attack on the Jewish people that nevertheless incorporated elements of traditional religious anti-Semitism.

Filippo often quoted the anti-Semitic writer Dr. Albérico Lagomarsino on this question. Lagomarsino shared Filippo's view of Freudianism, particularly regarding Jewish cultural and artistic activities. He asserted that various Jewish cultural entrepreneurs, by adopting "the psychoanalytic theory of Freud," promoted the "sublimation of the libido" into artistic expression. For Lagomarsino, psychoanalytic theory produced a specifically Jewish "artistic exhibition" that diluted the spirit and gave preeminence to the senses. The principles of corporeality and carnality represented a "step backward" in artistic forms. He denounced them as specifically Semitic traits while still exhibiting a certain quasi-pornographic fascination with the "impurities" of the psychoanalytic art promoted by the Jews. Tellingly, Lagomarsino used carnivalesque, even orgiastic, images to represent what he labeled "Jewish art." He described this art as characterized by indistinguishable naked bodies, "naked flesh in lascivious groups," a swarm of female bodies, lightweight clothing, disconnected members, and the manipulation of light and music. In short, for Lagomarsino, "coitus turns out to be the proposed theme. This is modern art under Jewish administration!"[3]

Filippo believed that unbridled sexual license was one of Freud's primary goals—that the father of psychoanalysis was resurrecting the Epicurean doctrines and thereby defending "free pleasure [libre gozo]" and constructing "a stairway" to descend into the "abuse of women" and the "ignominy of this century, the Judaic-Masonic-Communist discoveries." The ultimate consequence was "Freud's pretension to counteract God's influence in the corporeal world."[4] Filippo was not alone in his horror over the sexual aspects of the Jewish conspiracy that gathered together all those that Filippo deemed "adorers of Satan and the Phallus." Many Catholic anti-Semites suggested a secret relationship between Freud's supposed discursive assault on the truth of Christianity and the "cancer of the tongue" that Freud developed later in his life. The fascist priest Leonardo Castellani said that he heard this rumored when he visited Vienna in 1935.[5]

During the years of fascism, sexuality was central to Jewish stereotypes spread by the global anti-Semitic Right. Hitler himself projected his own fantasies and fears onto the sexual and racialized threat of Judaism.

With satanic joy in his face, the black-haired Jewish youth lurks in wait for the unsuspecting girl whom he defiles with his blood, thus stealing her from her people. With every means he tries to destroy the racial foundations of the people he has set out to subjugate. Just as he himself systematically ruins women and girls, he does not shrink back from pulling down the blood barriers for others, even on a large scale. It was and it is Jews who bring the Negroes into the Rhineland, always with the same secret thought and clear aim of ruining the hated white race by the necessarily resulting bastardization, throwing it down from its cultural and political height, and himself rising to be its master.[6]

While they shared some of Hitler's paranoid sexual fantasies, many Latin American fascists believed that he ignored the revealed Christian truth. However, for Argentine clerico-fascists the "Jewish problem" was still not merely theological but also racial. For Fr. Julio Meinvielle, the solution to the "problem" in Argentina had to be Catholic, not what eventually became the Nazi Final Solution.[7] For him, Nazi anti-Semitism was detached from superior political interests. And yet he also regarded Nazi violence as an outcome of God's global plan against the Left.[8] Given that Meinvielle accused the Jews of everything he didn't like, *nacionalista* violence could only be an anti-Semitic remedy. But this violence could not be pagan. For Meinvielle, there existed "a pagan mode that will reject the foreign because it's foreign; a Christian mode that will reject it in the measures in which it could be detrimental for the just interests of the country; a pagan mode that will reject and will hate the Jew because he is Jewish; a Christian mode that, knowing the solvent mission which the Jew occupies in the heart of Christian peoples, will limit his influence so that it doesn't cause harm."[9]

The Mexican fascist magazine *Timón* presented Hitler as fighting Jews in the name of truth, but his methods were not those of the "Catholic Majority of the world." The Mexican fascist Fernando de Euzcadi maintained that people could feel this "truth" in their spirit.

> The fact, however embarrassing it may seem, however humiliating it may be for the consciences, is in the spirit of all as a sad and disconsolate truth. And neither does humanity ignore the victim of the Jewish dictatorship, that the firm will, the emphatic energy of a patriot, is enough to destroy, to its foundations, the entire judaizing organization of a country. The Fuehrer of Magna Germany, who is a clairvoyant man of action, had no tremors in the pulse or weaknesses in the conscience. . . . The Jewish 'taboo' did not have force before the will of a man of iron solidly supported by his people.[10]

That said, Hitler was not an examplar for Latin America. De Euzcadi argued that "the Catholic world has other weapons: those of their faith, those of belief and the blush of the white man, of clean blood, before humiliation and renunciation." He stated that history was behind an "anti-Semitic crusade" that was not only "floating in the wind of a religion. It is the solid fencing of centuries of civilization, it is the fight for the convictions that we gently hear in the cradle of maternal lips. It is the gallantry of virility before the zigzagging baseness of the reptile." For those who believed these anti-Semitic lies, the stakes could not be higher: "To be or not to be: either Catholicism crushes Judaism, or Judaism by crushing Catholicism will drag with it the remains of two centuries of greatness stained by the mud of our cowardice and our diminished faith."[11]

But how could fascists fantasize that if their truth was so powerful Jews could crush it? Argentine fascists believed Freud and psychoanalysis were new powerful elements in a conspiratorial anti-Argentine alliance of Communists, Masons, and Jews. Filippo was an important mouthpiece for this ideological discourse during the 1930s. For fascists, there was a line in the sand that they would not cross: thus, the Jews were sexually abnormal and the fascists were not. Filippo found Freudianism's legitimization and reification of desire extremely problematic.[12] In turn, he coined a term for the part of the self that he wanted to be demoted, the "oneiric ego": "the ego of the inferior part, visceral and unconscious."[13] To Father Filippo it was clear that this "oneiric ego" was absolutely Jewish in its unmediated sexual, unconscious premises, whereas the "conscious ego" was purely Catholic and Argentine in its capacity to determine the will of individuals.

Thus, Filippo was committed to exposing Freud as an advocate of what he believed to be libidinal power. The famous psychoanalyst, like Albert Einstein, was a major figure in the framework of "dominant materialism" that, according to Filippo, undermined the national and Catholic capacity to master, by total repression, the disturbing forces of the unconscious.[14] Similarly, many Italian fascists identified a binary between the normal and the Jewish ego. For fascists, Freud had "submerged morality in the swamp of the libido."[15] In a symptomatic article titled "Down with Freud," the fascist Alberto Spaini referred to Freud as a false "Jewish pontiff" who put in question the immutability of the soul. Mussolini himself also referred to Freud as the "Maximus pontiff" of psychoanalysis.[16]

An interesting example of this depiction of psychoanalysis as attacking eternal truth was published in the Argentine Catholic journal *Criterio* by "Juan Palmetta," a pen name for Leonardo Castellani.

This priest mocked Freudian psychoanalysis. Castellani's insidious anti-Semitic humor is a window into the phobic world of this fascist interpretive community. For Castellani, Freudian "pansexualism" was an evident, almost given, fact that he labeled "Freudian sexology." He argued that this was a "damaging" alternative religion, with Freud as the "Holy Spirit."[17]

The idea of Freud questioning the immutability of souls and the truths they engendered and replacing them with his own sacred truth was intolerable to fascists. And yet it was notable that they were willing to engage with Freud to an extent on his own terms. Fascists stressed that Freud's theory of the unconscious had no place vis-à-vis the power of the mystical nature of the self. They saw the will as the expression of the soul and the producer of the truth. If their own version of the unconscious was the point of origin of their totalitarian voluntarism, they insisted that Freud made it seem to be an animal form outside history.

For the Brazilian Salgado, Freudian theory belonged to an artificial liberal past, namely, the nineteenth century. But it had now become a theory for communists, who were not really interested in workers but only in "Leninist demagoguery." They were "authentic bourgeois" who "boasted" of having found "the greatest novelty on the subject of philosophy, of sociology, of politics: Freud." Salgado contrasted Freudian theory to his own "Integralism," according to him "a conception absolutely rooted in the twentieth century." Unlike Freudian psychoanalysis, Brazilian fascism could not be understood by "*macacos* [monkeys], servile imitators, and passive taxpayers, by individuals unable to comprehend the time in which they live."[18] This fascist comprehension of time was deeply intuitive. In fascism, the race was "revealed" in the "intuition" and "intelligence of the subconscious." While psychoanalysis defended a theory of the unconscious as the "irruption of a primordial gorilla," fascism asserted and continuously made present the "primordial will to live."[19]

The fascist attack against psychoanalysis was done in the name of a subject without reason. It implied a domestication of the self and a denial of objective truth in the name of absolute truth. Fascists saw psychoanalysis as a significant threat because for them there was no tension between its democratic rejection of an eternal order of truth as dictated by the church or an authoritarian leader and its affirmation of the alienation of the bourgeois order. As Adorno observed in 1944, this was the perception of psychoanalysis displayed in "the fascist unconscious" of the terror magazines.[20]

In their interpretation of Freudian theory as a form of self-alienation, fascists defended the "man who celebrated his superiority" while denigrating "the Freudian man," the man of the libido. If the former epitomized a superior form of masculinity, uncontrolled and unreflexive sexual drives prevailed in the latter. For many fascists, psychoanalysis questioned the basic tenets of the fascist revolution, proposing alternate theories of history, truth, and myth. Fascists disputed the Freudian notion of the unconscious as "the depository of all the garbage of the spirit." For them, psychoanalysis proposed its own myths of transcendence and destruction. In a notable moment of projection, the fascist Alfonso Petrucci claimed that "the doctrine of the Jew Freud is new only in form and is part of the eternal fight of the subterranean world against that of light."[21]

For fascists, Freud wanted only "destruction." In contrast, the fascist revolution combined "destruction" and "construction." As the fascist professor Domenico Rende stated, the Freudian theory of the unconscious was "essentially against the fascist doctrine."

Fascists like Rende held the anti-Semitic view that only Jews could be the subject of abnormal behavior. Psychoanalysis was an outcome of the disease it was supposed to address, but fascism would "cure" non-Jews of psychoanalysis.[22] Many fascist fellow travelers agreed with these positions. For example, Carl Jung, formerly a disciple of Freud and then a member of the intellectual resistance against psychoanalysis, believed that the Jewish psyche—but not the "Aryan" psyche—should be controlled. For Jung, the Jewish unconscious was problematic, while the Aryan soul was a source of self-discovery and civilization. He saw German fascism as delving into its "depths."[23]

Fascism represented an attempt to blur the line between the inside and the outside, that is, to lift the barrier between the inner wishes of the mind and the external world. It was, in simple political terms, a rejection of reality checks. The fascists conceived their process as a form of radical historical agency, a fascist form of extreme historical voluntarism. For the Nazis, the primacy of the will encompassed a mythical historical continuum from darkness to light and from medieval settings to Hitler's modern leadership, as infamously dramatized at the beginning of Leni Riefenstahl's film *The Triumph of the Will*.[24] Both Nazism and fascism rooted their understanding of the national in a notion of the historical that often deviated from the historical record, precisely because it was full of mythic elements. For Italian fascists, Rome occupied (at least before the Italian racial laws of 1938) the same mythical dimension Nazism found in the imagined past of the race.

As the historian Saul Friedlander argues, "Nazism mobilized an apparently senseless set of images that nonetheless constantly evoked a longing for the sacred, the demonic, the primeval—in short, for the forces of myth."[25] But if for Freud myths functioned allegorically, as metaphors for the workings of the unconscious, fascism literalized myths as ideal expressions of the workings of the soul. Sorel emphasized these powerful political and analytical dimensions of mythical thinking.[26] Mussolini and Hitler went one step further; they not only used myths but also embraced them as superior truths, as sources for the act of fascist meaning-making.

9 Democracy and Dictatorship

A key fascist lie was the idea that dictatorship was the truest form of democracy. As with other fascist lies, this fabrication of "truth" replaced empirical truth. From the perspective of reality, the result of this kind of ideology could never be true. It was simply false. Nonetheless, fascists believed that their lies were evidence of deeper truths. They rejected real evidence and substituted it with a deep, almost religious faith in their leaders and the totalitarian ideology they defended. The leader and the ideology were, for them, the evidence that what they stood for represented an absolute truth. Fascists were not simply cynical about their lies. They wanted to believe in them, and they did.

Democracy was not an exception to this fascist pattern of combining lies with a deep belief in them. Inverting the terms of the equation, fascists identified existing democracy as a lie because they believed that electoral representation did not truly express the desires of the people. Only the leader could represent the people forever. For Hitler, as we might expect, the Jews were also behind this inherently false idea of a pluralistic democracy (i.e., a system that lacked a single will). Ironically, given this complaint, his rhetoric compressed all Jews into a unified willpower. Hitler spoke of the

Jews' supposed plan as that of a singular figure: "His ultimate goal in this stage is the victory of 'democracy', or as he understands it: the rule of parliamentarianism." In doing this Jews would replace "personality" with "the majority characterized by stupidity." Projecting his own intentions and desires, Hitler not only saw Jews as having a single evil plan; he actually said that they did not believe in democracy and wanted to establish a dictatorship. "Now begins the great last revolution," he wrote, forecasting the results of a radical Jewish plot. "In gaining political power the Jew casts off the few cloaks that he still wears. The 'democratic peoples' Jew becomes the blood-Jew and tyrant over peoples. In a few years he tries to exterminate the national intelligentsia and by robbing the peoples of their natural intellectual leadership makes them ripe for the slave's lot of permanent subjugation."[1]

In truth, of course, the fascists rejected liberal democracy and replaced it with dictatorship. The fascists also planned to exterminate their enemies, and, in time, they did. This displacement was practical as well as theoretical. As fascists argued, fascism was ontologically opposed to existing democratic life.[2] Fascism reified violent drives, presenting them as naked emanations of the true self. It was opaque, insofar as it represented something that could not be shared through either straightforward language or analogies. Instincts could only be expressed through acts of submission to the leader, who owned the truth.

From the United States to India, from Argentina to Japan, fascists argued that a real democracy never existed. They denounced parliamentarianism or maintained that it was old, or that it had been corrupted by communism, or that it was a Jewish plot. Nonetheless, they invented the idea that their authoritarianism would lead to a better, more functional, and truer form of democracy.[3] In China, the fascist Blue Shirts argued that existing democracy was the antithesis of the successful revolutionary movements that would "lay the foundation for a people's democracy."[4] Similarly, Spanish fascists denounced "the old lies of democracy" and identified popular sovereignty with the "doctrines and the procedures of redemptive fascism."[5]

In Mexico, the fascist intellectual José Vasconcelos argued that real modern democracy never existed. He editorialized, "Even the stones know already that democracy was buried the day when the main peoples of the time handed over their destinies, no longer to the freedom of suffrage, as in the small mediaeval republics of Italy or Spain, but to the Judeomasonic mafias who have been exploiting the eagerness and anguish, and innocence and misfortune of the nations. Democracy we have not seen, but we have seen imperialist intrigue and high plutocracy." Vasconcelos concluded that the absence of a real democracy meant that Nazi Germany represented the best possible power for Latin America's future. Like Hitler, he believed that Jews, especially American Jews, represented the true enemy of fascism, or, as he put it, they were "the same elements . . . that today in the United States preach the 'holy war' of international banking democracy against the liberating totalitarianism of Hitler and Mussolini."[6]

In Peru, fascists argued that as it existed democracy engendered "plutocracy" and could only be corrected by "proportional representation"; in France, they confronted "political democracy" with their aspiration to achieve a "democracy" that would be "integral" and "totalitarian."[7] In Argentina, Lugones described authoritarian rule as essentially antipolitical.[8]

Lugones advocated the reform of the electoral system in terms of corporative structures of government, what he, with self-proclaimed "impersonal objectivity," called "functional representation." Lugones argued that functional representation, with a universal but qualified vote organized in corporations and vocational groups, was the form of nationalism best adapted to the needs of Argentina. The people, as opposed to the "amorphous masses," would be the electors of this political system. Lugones identified ordinary politics with liberal democracy. He saw a corporatist system as part of the global fascist reaction against electoral representation but also diverged from Italian fascism in the sense that he wanted one corporation (the military) to reign supreme, even over the dictator. He considered this state to be transcendentally detached from politics as usual. This mythical dimension was at the root of his insistence on an "authoritarian reorganization [*reorganización autoritaria*]" of the state.[9]

Like the Mexican and Brazilian fascists, Lugones framed his proposed corporatist military state in the context of global fascism. For him, Mussolini was a "Machiavellian synthesis." Rather than being peculiarly Italian, fascism represented a universal pattern of "military democracies." The state's "reconcentration and defense" seemed to Lugones to be one of the basic tenets of Italian fascism. But they also were symptoms of broader dictatorial trends. Italian fascism was exemplary but not a model. Nonetheless, Italy's corporatist reality was truly important for Lugones. In his view, Mussolini had transformed Italy from a "proletarian and subaltern country" into a "potentate." This potency was the building block for the "creation of a new type of State."

Lugones saw fascism as he wanted it to be: a "democratic dictatorship."[10] In his mind fascism looked very similar to his own proposal for the Argentine state: a militaristic corporatist dictatorship, which he also symptomatically conceived as a military form of democracy.[11] Where antifascists simply saw a ruthless fascist dictatorship, many fascists believed that fascism was the only true democracy. This was, of course, a lie. But it is interesting that fascists really struggled to create a form of representation to replace constitutional democracy.

Delegation of power, and truth, in and to the leader was key. But this was not enough. For fascists, corporatism, as a legitimizing tool, could effectively bridge the contradiction between dictatorship and representation. Thus, they presented corporatism as the hallmark of democracy. Free and universal electoral representation would no longer be allowed. Corporatism was a crucial dimension of the defense against the supposed enemies of the nation: liberalism, communism, and Judaism. Democracy was in its "infancy," and fascism would bring it to maturity.[12]

All in all, fascists believed that corporatism provided substantial legitimacy to a dictatorial form of representation rooted in popular, if not electoral, sovereignty. In other words, for the fascists, true democracy was, in fact, a corporatist dictatorship.[13] Most fascists worldwide agreed that corporatism was an authoritarian form of democracy, a political regime that they also equated with the fascist form of dictatorship. They conceived of dictatorship as the only real form of political representation where dictators could arbitrate between different sectors of society and also where all people could obey the dictates of an autocratic executive power.

Corporatism was a key dimension of the global response to liberal democracy in the interwar period. To be sure, this idea had existed for many centuries, and it has not always been restricted to the antidemocratic camp or subordinated to the fascist notion of truth in politics.[14] As an ideological proposal, fascists came to associate corporatism with the absolute truths of their ideology. It was a constitutive part of the dictatorial alternative to liberal democracy, which many fascists saw as a mere prelude to communism.

This antiliberal and anticommunist version of corporatism was a major element in the global circulation of fascism.[15] While there are important doubts regarding the real application of corporatist practices, few historians will disagree about the centrality of corporatist ideas within fascist ideological circles and fascist regimes.[16]

Starting in the 1920s, corporatism increasingly became synonymous with antiliberal and anticommunist dictatorial forms of government. During this period, Mussolini included corporatism as a central element of fascist ideology. It was part of a "new synthesis" that "overcomes socialism and liberalism."[17] Mussolini was not alone. His corporatist "third way" between liberalism and socialism became a global vehicle for the diffusion and reformulation of fascist ideas. For fascist regimes, corporatism represented a form of sovereign legitimacy; it established a system of representation that did not downplay in any significant way the true authority of the dictator. In this situation corporatism provided a theory for regulating conflict under the supreme arbitration of the leader. If in nondictatorial forms of representation corporatism identified the state as the arbiter of interest groups, under totalitarian corporatism there was no difference between leader and state. In theory, corporatism worked ideologically for the legitimation of the dictator. It was supposed to demonstrate the truth of the power of people as incarnated in the leader. But in practice it never worked.

There was nothing democratic about fascist corporatism. Basically, one person ruled and everyone else was supposed to obey. Antifascists understood this clearly. In the 1920s, the famous legal thinker Hans Kelsen wrote that corporatism replaced the democratic form of parliamentary representation with a different form more akin to dictatorial rule. Kelsen argued against those who still believed that corporatism could enhance democracy. In fact, he demonstrated that the opposite was the case. Corporatism only served the interests of those who no longer identified with democratic constitutions. A desire for authoritarian domination was behind their opportunistic calls for the "organic" participation of all vocation groups in government. For Kelsen, corporatism was potentially dictatorial but intrinsically autocratic. It was always hostile to democracy.[18]

In contrast, for fascists, true corporatist democracy could not resemble the past. But what they understood as democracy, for all other observers was dictatorship. Why would dictators want to present dictatorship as democracy? Did they actually believe they were democratic? What is clear is that fascists needed democracy to be molded according to their ideological premises and expectations. Its truth was rooted in ideological imperatives, not reality. If the leader actually fully knew what the people wanted, then there would be real democracy. But this was clearly not the case, so dictatorship was constructed as democracy and democracy as it existed or had existed was presented as a fake vessel for evil plans that had to be destroyed. It had to be defeated in the name of ideological truth. Thus, the Spanish dictator Francisco Franco claimed that there were many definitions of democracy but only one "authentic one."[19] When Franco said, "In the new Spain, the democratic tradition will be preserved and, if possible, improved,"[20] was he simply lying? He later explained, "Confronting formal democracy, we oppose it with a practical democracy. . . . Our democracy gathers its desires and needs from the people."[21]

Across the world, fascists identified the existing liberal democracies with decadence and regarded them as, willingly or unwillingly, opening the gates to communism. The leader of the National Socialist Movement of Chile (the Chilean Nacis), Jorge Gonzalez von Marées, claimed that there was only a "pretense" of democracy in Chile. The fascists would "save democracy" by destroying the supposed democracy that was "feeding and strengthening the roots of Soviet dictatorship." In contrast to a communist dictatorship, the Chilean fascists maintained they wanted to create a "true democracy."[22]

Fascists identified constitutional democracies with a lie. They believed that it was not true that electoral representation could express popular sovereignty. For them, this idea was an "illusion."[23] Democracy imposed lies on the people and the nation. For Jean-Renaud, leader of the French Faisceau, democratic parliaments were the place representatives lost contact with "the real country," and also where they lost the "sense of truth."[24] Thus, for fascists, parliamentary democracy acted against the truth. Popular sovereignty could not be measured by democratic representation. Moreover, for fascists, democratic elections distorted true representation.

As the Argentine dictator José Felix Uriburu stated, "The word Democracy with a capital D no longer has meaning for us. . . . This doesn't imply that we are not democrats but more sincerely how much we hope that at some point a democracy in lowercase, but organic and truthful, replaces the dislocated demagogy that has done us great harm."[25] Uriburu was, above all, antiliberal. He wanted a dictatorial form of "democracy" rooted in corporatist forms of state organization. The Argentine dictator presented liberal democracy as a thing of the past. He warned those who believed "that the last word in politics is universal suffrage . . . as if there were nothing new under the sun[;] the corporations gave greatness and splendor to the Italian Communes of the twelfth and thirteenth centuries and degenerated later by the predominant action of the princes." Uriburu presented fascism as a novel actualization of a long-standing tradition: "The corporatist union is not a discovery of fascism but the modernized adaptation of a system whose results over a long epoch of history justify their resurgence."[26]

In fascism, elections were valid only if they confirmed dictatorship. Having decimated all opposition in the Spanish Civil War— half a million people were killed, and nearly as many went into exile—Franco called a referendum in 1947, confirming him as Head of State for life. Franco argued that this dubious election was extremely "free and welcoming." His ultimate lie was his argument that dictatorship and freedom were compatible. For Franco, antifascists were lying when they insisted that freedom was impossible under his rule. The enemy's lie had "such a virtuality, that it ends up deceiving the same ones that manufacture it by force of repeating it. Our triumph has overwhelmed them. However, no, we should not have great illusions. Malice is unforgiving, and we must be willing to defend, tenaciously and on all occasions, our truth."[27]

In 1938, Franco defended the fascists' lethal attack against Spanish democracy as being based on "arguments derived from the defense of the truth." Franco's place in the history of fascist lies did not escape the antifascist artist Pablo Picasso, who, shortly before completing his famous *Guernica* denouncing fascism and setting the record straight about its aerial killings of civilians, had published a small booklet with forceful etchings of the dictator, some of them related to his studies for the subsequent famous painting. The book was titled *Dream and Lie of Franco*. Picasso aptly saw the connections between the role that fascist lies and violence played in the figure of the dictator and the dictatorial methods he represented, on the one hand, and reality and experience, on the other.[28]

Fascists lies spared believers from engaging with the reality and suffering of those whose lives had been attacked and destroyed along with democracy.

The Spanish dictator projected onto his enemies the very mechanism that had allowed so many fascists to believe in the veracity of their own lies. This, of course, is a pattern we see repeated over time in the history of the fascist fabrication of truth.

10 The Forces of Destruction

In 1928, the French fascist Georges Valois wrote that under democracy two plus three equaled five but that in the new era of nationalist politics two plus three equaled six. What Valois meant is that under fascism a timeless truth would replace a logical truth. As he explained, in "bourgeois life, two and three make five. This is indisputable, according to the mercantile and legal spirit. In national life, two and three make six, because the heroic spirit changes."[1]

This spiritual change applied both to individuals and to the national community. The fascist revolution implied a radical transformation of the self according to the plan. Under fascism, heroic political forces were supposed to be unleashed. As we have seen, fascists searched for the unconscious as a project of self-realization. For them, the search for instincts could lead to disorder and chaos, but framed within fascism, it led to political domination. As the fascist intellectual Massimo Scaligero put it, fascism imposed "order" on the self by "bringing it from the plane of unconscious decadence and material darkness to the light of absolute reality, which is determined and deliberately constructed." This construction of reality was the result of an act of obedience to the ideology of the leader. Demonstrating the depths of this subordination, the fascist leader and education minister Giuseppe Bottai wrote to Mussolini in a personal letter, "I have put my own consciousness at the service of the leader." Fascists, according to their own logic, were not akin to "neurotics, the exalted, and those affected by egoistical sentimentalism." Fascist obedience represented the "translation" of the internal world of the unconscious into the absolute conscious order of fascism. It was an act of *forza*. It was the act of "command towards the self."[2]

Similarly, Leopoldo Lugones argued that life was marked by a "law of force." Truth was the outcome of power: "The truth constitutes a metaphysical entity, that is, a human ideation corresponding to various states of human information as well, which we call culture; and for this reason there were and always will be many religions and many philosophies." But Lugones was not a relativist: he saw all these "'religions and philosophies' as being subordinated to the 'instinct of domination.'" The fatherland was a result of this instinct to establish essential human hierarchies. Thus, it was "a phenomenon of natural history." Lugones understood his political realism as the emanation of "the concept of potency." Its limit was the same as the "capacity to impose a politics." For him this "politica realitas" was at work in the Roman Empire. Potency, the will to dominate others, was "the dynamic expression of sovereignty."[3]

Fascism demanded the exploration of the unconscious, its translation into politics, and the will to fight for a radical source of violence and authenticity. This fascist obsession with the role of violent desires in politics deeply preoccupied Freud and triggered a significant change in his theory of the unconscious. Despite the fascist emphasis on the dangers of the individualist psychoanalytic libido, for Freud, the libido was actually opposed to the damaging forces of the unconscious, what he called the "destructive instinct."

It was precisely during the years of fascism that Freud ascribed to the latter an overpowering autonomy from Eros. If before, Eros and Thanatos had worked more or less in tandem, fascism represented the loss of this weak stability. According to Freud's translator, James Strachey, it was because of fascism, and especially Hitler's actions, that Freud attributed increasing autonomy to "the human instinct of aggression and self-destruction."

In his 1930 seminal work, *Civilization and Its Discontents,* Freud highlighted the increasing political salience of destruction, an evolving domination that he saw in extremely pessimistic terms. He wrote, "Men have gained control over the forces of nature to such an extent that with their help they would have no difficulty in exterminating one another to the last man." In 1931 Freud added only one sentence to this previous paragraph, the last in the text. Regarding the ability of Eros to assert itself over destruction, Freud asked, "But who can foresee with what success and with what result?"[4] He saw this question as melancholically rhetorical. In a private letter in 1936, he wrote, "The world is becoming so sad that it is destined to speedy destruction."[5] In his response to an invitation to leave Vienna and settle in Buenos Aires in 1933, Freud described Nazism as a "German ignominy." More generally, he equated fascism with a brutal "education." Fascism represented a "retrogression into all but prehistoric barbarism."[6]

Fascism abhorred reason's attempt to repress intimate desires for political domination. In this sense, it was intuitively and almost dialectically opposed to Freud's interwar theory of the unconscious as well as to the critical arguments made by Hannah Arendt, José Carlos Mariátegui, Theodor Adorno, Max Horkheimer, Ernst Cassirer, Jorge Luis Borges, and many other contemporary antifascists.[7] In this context, one could argue that fascism's resistance to critical theory was essentially part of its prereflexive reaction to reason. This resistance was rooted in something that Antonio Gramsci, probably thinking about fascism, located within the realm of political fantasies about the self and its subordinated role in the collective: the centrality of mysticism and the sacred in the context of the political.[8]

Adorno concurred, noting how destruction was at the center of the psychological basis of the "fascist spirit." While fascist programs were "abstract and vague," fascist realizations were false and illusory. Fascism had profound archaic roots. It represented the "crude" transformation of Christian doctrine into slogans of "political violence." It involved revelation, sacrificial thoughts, simulation, and projection. Adorno distinguished here between leaders and followers. While the former often faked their religiosity and beliefs, he argued, the latter allowed themselves to be carried by lies. They simply wanted to religiously believe in the overpowering ego of the fascist leader. The leader confirmed his "basic identity" with followers based on innuendo. Then Adorno referred to "the role attributed by Freud to allusions in the interplay between the conscious and the unconscious." Leaders projected their desires onto enemies and followers alike. In turn, their primary aim was the fulfillment of their followers' repressed destructive desires.[9]

Desire and destruction (and the desire for destruction) were essential to the rise of fascism. The Peruvian antifascist thinker Mariátegui remarked that Mussolini had not created fascism; rather, "from a state of emotion, he extracted a political movement." He wondered how Mussolini could sound as convinced by fascism as he had been by socialism: "What was the mechanism of the process of conversion from one doctrine to the other? This is not a cerebral phenomenon. It is an irrational one. The engine behind this change in ideological attitude was not the idea. It was the sentiment."[10]

In fact, as early as 1914 Mussolini had identified his departure from socialism as a result of the need to follow "the new truth." The future leader had identified this sacred truth with violence.[11] Mariátegui agreed that Mussolini had consciously decided to leave behind socialism and embrace the fascist "cult of violence." But Mariátegui did not believe that this new politics was the result of a personal evolution. Mussolini's new faith had been dictated by his followers. They expected a particular reality from him, and he delivered. "His ideological consubstantiation" was a result of his decision to identify with the expectations of his fascist followers.[12]

Gramsci, Adorno, and Mariátegui, like Arendt and others, were not ultimately willing to believe that fascists really and rationally meant what they said. Yet fascism enacted a "theory of self" based on the political role of the unconscious. Fascism equated this passage from unconsciousness to consciousness with the disclosure of transcendental truths. For Adorno, this notion of the truth was dually rooted in the fetishization of reality and of established power relations. Fascism equated what was right with redemptive notions of salvation. The leader dreamed "a union of the horrible and the wonderful." The result was not only the death and destruction of the enemy but also the self. The structure of fascism was embedded in the "unconscious psychological desire for self-annihilation." Adorno warned his readers that although Hitler's speeches were "insincere," cultivated people were mistaken in refusing to take them seriously.[13] Arendt also stressed the allusive dimension of fascism. Nazi lies "alluded to certain fundamental truths," believed by "gullible Europeans," and led them into the "maelstrom" of "destruction itself."[14]

While many antifascists described fascism as seeking to impersonate ridiculous atavisms, fascists searched for the perceived archaic dimensions of the self. They saw in them the original nucleus of the truth. This is the reading that Borges stressed in his critical analysis of fascism during the interwar years. He also saw fascism as "sentimental." But he went further. Fascism was a collection of political subjects who were, impossibly, studying to be barbarians. Fascism wanted to establish a new "morality." Their full trust in the leader, the "idolatrous adoration of the *jefes*," led fascists to believe in magic and the reification of total violence. In 1938, Borges argued, "Fascism is a state of the soul. In fact, it does not require from its proselytized followers more than the exaggeration of certain patriotic and racial prejudices that all people have."[15]

Fascists wanted to leave reason behind and return to prejudice. Borges stressed that fascists were engaged in a form of thinking that represented the antithesis of reason. He called it "monstrous reason." This "reason" wanted to rest its authority on the representation of the inner self, but, in fact, fascism could only present itself as "impulsive and illogical."[16] Notoriously, the fascist return of the repressed was a conscious act. In practice, and far from occurring intuitively, fascist self-immersion led to a doctrine of destruction. Fascist self-consciousness led to the equation of power, truth, and violence.

As conceived in a fascist key, consciousness represented a desired assertion of true sovereignty. Mussolini articulated this thesis in 1925, explaining that in fascism a generic population became "a conscious people." For the Duce, this was the moment when "the truth of history became the bread of the conscious spirit of Italians."[17] At this point history was turned into myth. Its aim was the destruction of any trace of demonstrable truth.

Epilogue

The Populist War against History

Whether writing his memoirs in Argentina or in Jerusalem, whether speaking to the police examiner or to the court, what he said was always the same, expressed in the same words. The longer one listened to him, the more obvious it became that his inability to speak was closely connected with an inability to think, namely, to think from the standpoint of somebody else. No communication was possible with him, not because he lied but because he was surrounded by the most reliable of all safeguards against the words and the presence of others, and hence against reality as such.

HANNAH ARENDT, *Eichmann in Jerusalem*

For decades, populist leaders have been both destroying the historical record in a literal sense and playing with the memory and experiences of the victims of fascism, all for political gain. Their actions are part of a deeper pattern that confuses lies with truth. The rise of Trumpism in 2016 revealed little that was new, but the fact that populism now ruled the most powerful country on earth brought this problem to the forefront. According to the *Washington Post,* President Trump's record of lying puts him in a different league from other politicians. As the newspaper put it, "It's (almost) official: The president of the United States is a liar." In more diplomatic terms, the *New York Times* observed that there is one "truth about his presidency: Bad news about him is fake until he says otherwise." Many of his critics even wondered whether he had a reached an Orwellian level of lying.[1] Orwell observed in his novel 1984, "The party told you to reject the evidence of your eyes and ears. It was their final, most essential command."[2]

The ascription of this literary dimension to Trumpism illuminates the connections between the history of fascist lies analyzed in this book and the present. Trumpism has already achieved a prominent place in the history of political lying. More specifically, it embodies a new chapter in a longer history that connects interwar fascism to contemporary populism. Trumpism clearly belongs to the long history of the fabrication of alternative truth, a "truth" relying on the insights and desires of the leader.

As with Mussolini's and Hitler's conflation of the truth with the leader's infallibility, Trumpism embraced the idea that the leading light of the movement embodied a divine nature, that he was a man different from all other men. He was not only, as he immodestly put it, "so great looking and smart, a true Stable Genius!" but also, as the White House press secretary Sarah Sanders suggested, a hand of God. As Sanders put it, "I think God calls all of us to fill different roles at different times, and I think that he wanted Donald Trump to become president and that's why he's there." Trump himself identified his politics with a religious mandate, even claiming a relation between legality, the state, and the divine: "Our rights are not given to us by men; our rights are given to us from our creator. . . . No matter what, no earthly force can take those rights away." The anti-Semitic trope that American Jews are disloyal to the country was restated by Trump when he claimed in an interview that Jews who vote Democratic were showing "either a total lack of knowledge or great disloyalty." According to this logic, by ignoring or betraying the truth of the leader, American Jews were unfaithful in both religious and political terms. Later, he doubled down on his stance, thanking a right-wing conspiracy theorist on Twitter for claiming that Israelis "love [Trump] like he is the second coming of god." God and the metaphor of Trump as a god were conflated in Trumpism. When asked about God, Trump himself responded by praising the Lord and his own persona, business deals, and leadership. More directly, Trump's campaign manager stated the president was sent by God to save the country.[3] The amalgamation of the leader with God became an article of religion for Trumpists, as had been the case with fascists.

Mussolini relied on this idea of divine inspiration to state the most outrageous lies. As we have seen, fascist propaganda asserted that the fascist leader was always right. Hitler made this link with the divine even more explicit; although Hitler rarely credited any source of inspiration outside of his own genius, as a man he modeled himself on the pope. The Führer asserted, "I hereby set forth for myself and my successors in the leadership of the Party the claim of political infallibility. I hope the world will grow as accustomed to that claim as it has to the claim of the Holy Father."[4]

Goebbels, the master of propaganda who helped turn Hitler into a living myth, actually believed that Hitler was a "genius" and had been sent by God to save Germany. Fascist propaganda delivered and even created its own proof of success. Even Goebbels's "own diaries, which were to be published posthumously, were also intended to form part of the documentation of his success."[5] There was no difference between documentation and fabrication.

Nazi propaganda forged a myth of Hitler that could not be factually proven, namely, that he was a god that had descended from the sky. But the Nazis did not literally think this. Like everybody else, they could see that their leader had landed in an airplane. Nonetheless, for them, the descent of Hitler was a metaphor drawn from the ultimate truth of ideology. They believed in its reality. Images of Hitler, whether in movies like *The Triumph of the Will* or in state propaganda, were metaphors of a faith, a truth that was beyond the need for proof.

How far is the populist world of Trumpism from the fascist fusion of infallibility, the truth, and God? In fact, many Americans believed that Trump's electoral college victory was God's work. As one of Trump's Christian supporters argued, "Millions of Americans . . . believe the election of President Trump represented God giving us another chance—perhaps our last chance to truly make America great again."[6] Trump himself seemed to believe in his own myth. He believed in his "great and unmatched wisdom." He could never be wrong. Typically, when asked in 2019 about a lie that he had told regarding Russia and Venezuela, Trump responded that if reality did not correspond to his statements now, they would soon become the truth. His reasoning did not depend on any sort of empirical evidence but on a belief in his innate and absolute trustworthiness. Arguing with journalists in the Oval Office, Trump said, "Well, let's just see who's right." He asked them, "Do you know what you're going to do? You're going to see in the end who's right, okay? You just watch it. Okay? And we'll see who's right. Ultimately, I'm always right."[7]

The idea that the unmediated, and unquestioned, voice of the leader represents the truth works in tandem with the fantasy that traditional media has nothing to offer the public except lies. The falsehoods about the extent of fraud whenever the president did not like electoral or polling results are crucial to this Trumpist history of lies.

As a presidential candidate in 2016, Donald Trump refused to commit to accepting the results if he lost the election. After winning the election, Trump argued on multiple occasions that Hillary Clinton had won the popular vote only because of illegal voting, a charge that had no evidence. As a former White House counsel put it, "He then established a commission co-chaired by Vice President Pence and Kansas Secretary of State Kris Kobach to study voter fraud, but after it failed to turn up evidence of illegal voting and was successfully sued by one of its own members for operating illegally, it was abruptly disbanded."[8] Trump lied that he lost New Hampshire because of the fraud executed by liberal voters from Massachusetts. He lied about the connections between his presidential campaign and Russia.

But perhaps the most obvious lie of all was the one regarding the historical nature of his victory. He argued that "Democrats . . . suffered one of the greatest defeats in the history of politics in this country." As NPR showed, Trump's contention about the historical nature of his victory (and his enemy's defeat) was contradicted by the actual results: "Trump won 306 electoral votes to Clinton's 232. . . . But it's hard to argue this represents a landslide of historic proportions, given that out of 58 presidential elections, the winner has received more electoral votes in 37 contests."[9] Lying about history became central to Trump's construction of the truth.

Why is Trump so obsessed with and why has he lied so many times about issues to do with his election? Historically, populism turns elections into a plebiscitarian confirmation of an ideological truth about the leader. After winning them, populism pretends that its elected leader impersonates the people and is their only true representative. Elections constitute the essence of legitimation because they act to confirm the sovereignty of the populist caudillo.

In this sense, populism is very different from fascism, where there is no place for meaningful elections.[10]

. . .

Fascism and populism both appeal to the political trinity, leader, nation, and people, as their main source of legitimation. In both formations, there is no contradiction between the people, the nation, and the representation of the people in the persona of the leader. These ideologies believe in personification as representation, which means, in effect, that achieving the will of the people is fully delegated to the leader. This three-part myth of representation rests on the fantasy that somehow a single leader is the same as a nation and its people—an identification of one person and two concepts. In fascism, however, this personification did not require any rational or procedural mediation, such as electoral representation.[11] In contrast, in populism, elections are important in confirming the truth of the divine supremacy of the leader, and spreading lies about them is a crucial part of maintaining the leader's idea of his place in history.

By winning plebiscitary elections the populist leader confirms the dual nature of his power; he is at the same time an elected representative and a quasi-transcendental conductor of people. As Perón often said, "The people should know . . . that the conductor is born. He is not made, not by decree nor by elections." He added, "It is essential that the conductor finds his own molds, to later fill them with a content that will be in direct relation, according to his efficiency, with the sacred oil of Samuel that the conductor has received from God."[12]

The idea of eternal incarnation led in fascism, and leads in populism, to the proclamation of the leader's infallibility, even to the extent that the selection of the leader represents the last opportunity for the nation. This sense of emergency and imminent danger to the nation and the people is a result of the leader's projection of friend-enemy positions and military strategies onto the intentions of his opponents. As then-candidate Trump claimed, referring to the upcoming presidential election of 2016, "For them [his enemies] it's a war, and for them nothing at all is out of bounds. This is a struggle for the survival of our nation, believe me. And this will be our last chance to save it on November 8—remember that." Trump told his followers that his election marked "our independence day." Perón similarly identified his own election in 1946 with a second "independence," maintaining, "God put me on earth for the independence and the freedom of the Argentine people." He also identified his leadership with a long history of military conquerors who were, like him, conductors of the people: "The history of the world, through the examples of Alexander, Julius Caesar, Frederick or Napoleon, shows that victory belongs to those that know to lift and conduct the people."[13]

If when modern populism gained power after 1945 it reformulated fascism in a democratic key, the new populists of the contemporary Right are getting closer to the fascist dream of the destruction of history and its replacement with the myth of the infallible leader. Early populist leaders had a certain hesitation about radically changing the historical record, as the fascists had done. This has changed with the right-wing populists of this new century. They are reverse engineering their own history, especially with respect to the history of fascism itself.

The distortion of fascist history in general, and Nazi history in particular, has been a fundamental feature of the new populist brand. Israeli Prime Minister Benjamin Netanyahu, at times allied with racist and xenophobic parties in Israel and abroad, has also distorted Holocaust history to suit his political interests, most recently by suggesting that an interwar pro-Nazi Palestinian leader was a key actor in the extermination of European Jews. According to Netanyahu, in 1941 Adolf Hitler asked the mufti's advice: "What should I do with them?" The mufti replied, "Burn them."[14] There is no evidence that this dialogue ever took place. Similarly, the American caudillo Donald Trump denounced his enemies for supposedly adopting Gestapo tactics but also attacked "anti-fa" and claimed that even among neo-Nazis there were "good people."[15]

Why do populist leaders want to forgive, distort, or displace the actual history of Nazism and fascism? Because, as these leaders draw from the well of fascist ideology, rhetoric, and tactics, they have to neuter the history of fascism to normalize their politics. Revising the history of fascism renders it mythical rather than historical, suggesting that the fascism of the past was not that bad—or not even fascism at all. This is, of course, a lie.

Rewriting history is therefore central to the populist project. In Brazil, President Jair Bolsonaro is doing this not just with the Nazi past but with his own country's history as well. For those worried about Bolsonaro's defense of political violence and desire to expand the powers of the presidency, his push to whitewash the country's dictatorial past was symptomatic of a larger pattern of populist lying about history—and deeply troubling.

In 2019, Bolsonaro wanted to officially celebrate the 1964 coup that led to the most murderous military dictatorship in Brazil's history. Moreover, he falsely claimed that this dictatorship had established democracy in Brazil, even arguing that it had not really been a dictatorship. In 2018, Bolsonaro talked with Viktor Orban, the autocratic and racist populist leader of Hungary, and claimed that the

Brazilian people did not know what a dictatorship is, suggesting that the military junta that ran the country from 1964 to 1985 could not be classified this way. This attempt was no different from the classic fascist lie that fascist dictatorships were true forms of democracy. Like the historians of fascism who laid these lies to rest, historians of Brazil who have studied the authoritarian regime have shown the opposite. And according to the Brazilian Truth Commission, the Brazilian dictatorship that Bolsonaro wanted to commemorate was responsible for, among other things, 434 deaths and disappearances of its opponents, as well as the massacre of more than 8,000 native people.

Bolsonaro's normalization, even celebration, of a deadly regime was not just limited to his take on Brazilian history. He heaped praise on several dictators, including the Chilean president Augusto Pinochet, who was arrested for numerous human rights violations, and the Paraguayan president Alfredo Stroessner, who kept the nation under martial law for almost all of his thirty-five years in power. By claiming these dictators were their countries' saviors, leaders like Bolsonaro and Trump replace history with myth. The past has become an indispensable part of what Hannah Arendt identified as the fabrication and centralization of lying. As I cited in the epigraph to this chapter, for Arendt, when followers become believers of these lies, they are unable to regard reality as such. In this context, politicians use "deliberate falsehood as a weapon against the truth."[16] As the historian Ruth Ben-Ghiat observed regarding Trump's deep connection with the propaganda machines of authoritarian states in the past, "Since taking office, Trump has set up an information apparatus that presents him and his loyalists as the only arbiters of truth and that labels critics as partisan purveyors of falsity."[17] In this revisionist world the most irrational, messianic, and paranoid views are falsely presented as history.

Like Trump's, Bolsonaro's style and substance, steeped in political violence, national chauvinism, and personal glorification, have essential fascist hallmarks. But it is his manipulation of history that truly reveals how the Bolsonaro regime links populism to fascism. He has unabashedly used history as a mere propaganda tool. His decision to celebrate the 1964 coup was reminiscent of classic fascists like Hitler and Mussolini who, after being selected and appointed to lead coalition governments, destroyed democracy from within. As rulers, they invented a mythical past that identified emperors and heroic warriors as mere predecessors of their rule. Perhaps with less grandiosity than the Duce and the Führer, Bolsonaro aimed to link his own rule with that of the Latin American dictators of the past. If the fascist leaders created a myth of fascism that established them as living incarnations of an invented golden past, Bolsonaro invented and then sought to personify a mythical age of Latin American dictatorships. It is yet unclear how far down the path from populism to fascism Bolsonaro will go. Right-wing populists like Bolsonaro do not automatically translate their radical rhetoric and celebration of the memories of fascism and dictatorship into fascist or dictatorial practices. Of course, populists like Bolsonaro, Orban, Trump, and Italy's Matteo Salvini execute policies of discrimination, violence, and increasing inequality. But so far they have done this without entirely breaking democracy. Their most antidemocratic moves are symbolic. Attacks on political enemies do not generally—so far—move beyond words. Here lies a difference between fascism and populism. The populist leaders favor violent rhetoric, and lies about the self and the enemy, without backing them up with violent action. As General Juan Domingo Perón, the first populist to come to power after the fall of fascism in 1945, stated, he was an "herbivorous lion."[18]

Is Bolsonaro also this kind of peaceful lion, willing to roar but not to devour? And is this also the case with Trump? Or are they true lions of fascism? In a statement that Trump tweeted and praised, Mussolini said that "it is better to live one day as a lion than 100 years as a sheep." In a similar vein, Goebbels presented Hitler as a "lion, roaring, great, and gigantic." The figure of the lion meant that fighting and killing, in either civil war or war between nations, were key, unavoidable dimensions of politics. These ideas of violence and war were intimately related to the religious faith that these leaders demanded of their followers, using symbols and language from Christian texts and liturgy to depict themselves as modern-day redeemers. This is one reason that perceptions of persecution emboldened them.

By feeding the savior or martyr image he wants to construct, Trump presents himself as the most persecuted leader in history and relishes the opportunity to complain that any investigation into his alleged crimes is a "witch-hunt" or harassment. In 2019, in the context of a congressional impeachment inquiry, Trump approvingly tweeted the comments of a pastor who warned, "If the Democrats are successful in removing the President from office (which they will never be), it will cause a Civil War like fracture in this Nation from which our Country will never heal."[19] The apocalyptic views of the Trumpist pastor are widely shared among Trump's most fanatic followers. The attachment to the leader's "truth" seems so secure that it transcends ethics and common sense—and justifies his most offensive and apparently illegal acts. Like Trump and his fascist predecessors, Bolsonaro sees civil war as a political ideal.[20] This idea of politics as the site for an all-or-nothing pseudoreligious war between the sacred truth and the lies of a demonic enemy explains why political violence is preferable to the leader's electoral defeat. While Mussolini had stated that "fascism believes in the sanctity of heroism," Bolsonaro's followers literally call him "myth" and consider him a hero of epic proportions, a Christian warrior of patriotism and family values who needs to be trusted without question. After winning the election in 2018, Bolsonaro told Brazilians, "We need to get used to living with the truth. There is no other way. Thanks to God, this truth was understood by the Brazilian people." He fully identified with this transcendental truth because he was going to fulfill "God's mission."[21] Bolsonaro clearly stands on the border between fascist dictatorship and the democratic form of populism. When he wants to celebrate dictatorship and whitewash the Nazi past, he looks very little like classic populists like Perón and much more like Hitler and Mussolini. Similar things might be said about Trump's celebration of calls to shoot migrants or his serial racist remarks and actions against Hispanics, Muslims, and other minorities.

The background in all these cases is a notion of truth fully embedded in a longer history of fascist lies. What Trump, for example, believes to be the truth is a mere lie. Because of this refusal to accept reality as it is, he and many other leaders have been mistakenly branded as deranged.[22] The idea of denouncing such a leader as insane is also not new. Populist and fascist leaders have often been called crazy. But rather than accurately diagnosing the situation, this view reflects the confusion of an opposition faced with an unusual form of politics that renders truths into lies and lies intro truths—a confusion that historically has led to inaction vis-à-vis authoritarianism and its intolerant consequences.

Adolf Hitler was treated by many of his opponents as a crazy liar. This conceptual laziness, perpetuated by so many antifascists at the time of the Holocaust, contributed to Nazi success. By dismissing Hitler as a pathetic, impulsive charlatan, they could ignore that he coldly planned war and genocide while generating a wide consensus about these among the German population. As Hitler created new realities, he made the world look more and more like the lies he was telling.

More generally, the presentation of these leaders as ridiculous deceivers, an idea fixed on their style and not on the deeply violent and racist ideological content of their message, proved to be a distraction from the real consequences of their practices and politics. This misconception of fascist leaders as deranged also worked, inaccurately, to separate the "abnormal" leaders from their supposedly confused but sane followers. And it divorced political ideology, including racism and anti-Semitism, as well as fascist lies, from political analysis, resulting in an inability to mount a clear and effective opposition to these leaders' agenda.

This tendency to use mental illness or a psychiatric disorder as an explanation for the lies and actions of such leaders adds to the general misunderstanding of what makes them successful: a narcissistic drive that establishes them as godlike genius figures, absolute voices of the people who know better than the people themselves what they, the people, truly want. They own the "truth," a truth that has nothing to do with corroboration and empirical demonstration.[23]

Presenting irrational leaders as insane, as swindlers, or both, scores easy political points. But in the long term, a focus on the insanity of the mythomaniac leader, rather than on his and his followers' mythic ideology, overshadows the most important fact about their leadership: the reality that their fundamentally authoritarian lies and racist fantasies about the world become constantly normalized and supported by a wide segment of the people, as well as major party figures. Trump was probably right in assuming that many of his followers share his racist belief that Haiti and African nations are "shithole countries."[24] Although Trumpism does have key intolerant and antidemocratic dimensions, there is nothing new or pathological about this. The history of populists in power, from Juan Perón to Silvio Berlusconi, and of fascist leaders like Hitler and Mussolini before them, is full of self-aggrandizing and mythmaking tendencies—tendencies that were fully supported and sometimes initiated by their parties and followers.

Dismissive and simple explanations about the stupidity of authoritarian fraudsters and their gullible followers do not actually explain much. Instead, they are symptomatic of a refusal to understand what we might not like: the mythical incarnation of truth that leads to its decimation. Trump is an extreme populist with a xenophobic anti-egalitarian agenda. Programmatic politics and winning elections against him are more important to the present and future of democratic life than assessing his psychiatric state or stereotyping him as a con man. He does not lie because he is a crazy cheater; he lies because he belongs to a political tradition that proposes an alternative notion of truth that emanates from the sacred infallibility of the leader. The racism and misogyny springing from the White House are political, attempts to transform reality in order to make it closer to fantasy. This cannot be ignored.

Moreover, we should ask ourselves why the critiques of authoritarian populists often do not go beyond the simplistic use of adjectives, even insults. *Abnormalizing* Trump normalizes the rest of the American landscape, as if Trump is a parenthetical aside in an unblemished history of pluralism, equality, and respect for historical truth. This was never the case in the United States, any more than it has been in the rest of the world. In fact, the forms of extreme right-wing populism that emerged during the Cold War

(McCarthyism and later the presidential candidacies of Barry Goldwater and George Wallace) are key American antecedents for understanding the appeal of Trump's repressive ideas, racist lies, and authoritarian style.

Globally, Trumpist mythmaking has a history that includes populists and fascist leaders like Juan Perón in Argentina and Getulio Vargas in Brazil in the early postwar period and, more recently, Hugo Chávez and Nicolás Maduro in Venezuela. As a modern populism in power, Trumpism represents an extreme form of postfascism, an antiliberal, and often anticonstitutional, authoritarian democracy with a political rationale of its own. This is a political formation with a mythical notion of the truth. Like the fascists, populists replace historical truth with fake ideas about a glorious past that their leaders promise to revive. This is the context for understanding the historical emptiness of an expression such as "Make America Great Again." The leader restores to life a past that never existed. This was at the center of the fascist fabrication of the truth. It is also a crucial driver of modern right-wing populism.

Will the rise of leaders like Bolsonaro, Trump, and Orban lead to a twenty-first-century fascism? It is not yet clear. It is probably (and hopefully) unlikely that such a political turn will happen, but these politicians' troubling embrace of increasingly extreme mythical lies should be a signal to those who believe in democracy that they must resist rising illiberalism and renewed fascist impulses not only with votes and demonstrations but also with a defense of history.

Acknowledgments

This small book is the result of many conversations in many countries. I first presented its main argument as a series of lectures at the University of Macerata in 2013 and then elaborated it over the years on three continents. I want to thank the students of that dear Italian university as well as my students at the New School in New York. I want to thank also Amy Allen, Ben Brower, Amy Chazkel, Valeria Galimi, Luis Herrán Ávila, Aaron Jakes, Andrea Mammone, Nara Milanich, Pablo Piccato, Caterina Pizzigoni, and Angelo Ventrone for their comments and suggestions on different parts of the book. I also want to thank Giulia Albanese, Melissa Amezcua, Andrew Arato, Borja Bauzá, Chiara Bottici, Richard Bernstein, Fabián Bosoer, Magdalena Broquetas, Antonio Costa Pinto, Donatella Di Cesare, Richard Evans, Oz Frankel, Maximiliamo Fuentes Codera, Fabio Gentile, Emmanuel Guerisoli, the late Agnes Heller, Reto Hofmann, Andreas Kalyvas, Claudia Koonz, Daniel Kressel, Dominick LaCapra, Simon Levis Sullam, Sandra McGee Deutsch, David Motadel, Jose Moya, Julia Ott, Elias Palti, Raanan Rein, Sven Reichardt, Daniel Rodriguez, Gema Santamaria, Hector Raul Solis Gadea, Michael Steinberg, Ann Laura Stoler, Nathan Stoltzfus, Alberto Spektorowski, Enzo Traverso, Nadia Urbinati, Jeremy Varon, and Nikolai Wehrs.

My deep thanks to Kate Marshall, my ideal editor at UC Press. At UC Press, my appreciation also goes to Tim Sullivan, director of the press; Enrique Ochoa; Dore Brown; and Sheila Berg, for her acute and perceptive copyediting. I also thank Emmanuel Guerisoli for preparing the index.

My thanks to my parents, Norma and Jaime, and my siblings, Inés and Diego. As always I owe the deepest gratitude to my wife, Laura, and my daughters, Gabriela and Lucia.

. . .

A signficantly shorter Italian version of the book was published in 2019 by EUM. Parts of the book were published in very different form in the journals *Constellations* (2016) and *Hispanic American Historical Review* (2007).

Notes

Preface

1. I have taken some of these reflections from articles that I wrote or cowrote in these past two years. See "The Danger of President Trump's Lies Amid the Coronavirus and Urban Uprisings," *Washington Post*, June 3, 2020; "La mentira racista tiene consecuencias," *El País* (Spain), May 29, 2020; "Mirada desde el centro de la pandemia" (with Laura Palermo), *Clarín* (Argentina), March 22, 2020; "A Covid Genocide in the Americas?" (with Jason Stanley), Project Syndicate, January 18, 2021; "The Fascist Politics of the Pandemic" (with Jason Stanley), Project Syndicate, May 4, 2020; "Coronavirus, mentiras y muerte," *Agenda Pública/El País* (Spain), March 21, 2020; "El coronavirus y la tentación autoritaria" (with Laura Palermo), *Agenda Pública/El País* (Spain), February 26, 2020. On Orbán, see comments by Kim Scheppele in Elisabeth Zerofsky, "How Viktor Orbán Used the Coronavirus to Seize More Power," *New Yorker*, April 9, 2020.

2. www.politico.com/news/2020/09/26/joe-biden-trump-joseph-goebbels-422047.

Introduction

The chapter epigraphs are from the following sources: Donald J. Trump, quoted in Philip Bump, "A New Peak in Trump's Efforts to Foster Misinformation," Washington Post, July 25, 2018; Adolf Hitler, in *Hitler: Speeches and Proclamations, 1932–1945,* ed. Max Domarus (London: Tauris, 1990), 2489; Benito

Mussolini, in Benito Mussolini, *Opera omnia,* ed. Edoardo and Duilio Susmel (Florence: La Fenice, 1951–62), vol. 19, 114.

1. Max Horkheimer, *Between Philosophy and Social Science* (Cambridge, MA: MIT Press, 1993), 278.

2. See Hannah Arendt, "Truth and Politics," *New Yorker,* February 25, 1967; Alexandre Koyré, "The Political Function of the Modern Lie," *Contemporary Jewish Record* 8 (1945): 290–300; Agnes Heller, *La verità in politica* (Rome: Castelvecchi, 2019); Jacques Derrida, *Historia de la mentira: Prolegómenos* (Buenos Aires: Universidad de Buenos Aires, Facultad de Filosofía y Letras, 1995). See also Martin Jay, *The Virtues of Mendacity: On Lying in Politics* (Charlottesville: University of Virginia Press, 2010); Timothy Snyder, *The Road to Unfreedom* (New York: Tim Duggan Books, 2018).

3. "In Texas Gunman's Manifesto, an Echo of Trump's Language," *New York Times,* August 5, 2019.

4. See Jason Stanley, *How Fascism Works* (New York: Random House, 2018), 56. On Trumpist language and Nazism, see Michelle Moyd and Yuliya Komska, "Donald Trump Is Changing Our Language. We Need a Vocabulary of Resistance," *The Guardian,* January 7, 2017.

5. See Federico Finchelstein, "Why Far-Right Populists Are at War with History," *Washington Post,* April 23, 2019; Federico Finchelstein, "Cuando el populismo potencia al fascismo," *New York Times Es,* May 21, 2019; Federico Finchelstein, "Jair Bolsonaro's Model Isn't Berlusconi. It's Goebbels," *Foreign Policy,* October 5, 2018.

6. Ishaan Tharoor, "Trump Goes Soft on Terrorism," *Washington Post,* August 6, 2019.

7. See my preface to the paperback edition of *From Fascism to Populism in History* (Oakland: University of California Press, 2019), xvii–xix.

8. As Joan Wallach Scott observed, "Trump insists, in typical demagogic fashion, that his lies are self-evident truths. His followers find some inherent, deeper truth in those lies. And he elicits from them a populist energy that lacks any social consciousness or social responsibility." Joan Wallach Scott, "Political Concepts: A Critical Lexicon," www.politicalconcepts.org/trump-joan-wallach-scott/#ref20.

9. See James Q. Whitman, *Hitler's American Model: The United States and the Making of Nazi Race Law* (Princeton, NJ: Princeton University Press, 2017).

10. Jonathan Watts, "Amazon Deforestation: Bolsonaro Government Accused of Seeking to Sow Doubt over Data," *The Guardian*, July 31, 2019; Ernesto Londoño, "Bolsonaro Fires Head of Agency Tracking Amazon Deforestation in Brazil," *New York Times*, August 2, 2019. Later, at the United Nations, Bolsonaro denied that the Amazon was deeply affected by the massive fires that his own actions (or rather, inactions) provoked. He stopped short of denying the fires themselves, unlike Trump, who invented a hurricane in Alabama in the so-called Sharpiegate.

11. On myth and fascism, see my book *El mito del fascismo: De Freud a Borges* (Buenos Aires: Capital Intelectual, 2015).

1. On Fascist Lies

Chapter epigraph: "A alguno de esos mentirosos precisos le di con el puño en la cara. Los testigos aprobaron mi desahogo, y fabricaron otras mentiras. No las creí, pero no me atreví a desoírlas." Jorge Luis Borges, "El hombre en el umbral," in *Obras completas* I (Barcelona: Emecé, 1996), 613.

1. Hitler, and also Goebbels, insisted that propaganda needs constant repetition, but they never argued that they were telling lies. In fact, they believed the opposite, that they spoke in the name of truth. Fascists typically deny what they are and ascribe their own features and their own totalitarian politics to their enemies. Thus, Goebbels never said that repeating lies was central to Nazism, but he did say, in 1941, regarding "Churchill's lie factory," that "the English go by the principle that if you lie, then lie, and above all, stick to what you have lied." In 1942 he wrote in his private diary that "the essence of propaganda is simplicity and repetition." See http://falschzitate.blogspot.com/2017/12/eine-luge-muss-nur-oft-genung-wiederholt.html. See also Leonard W. Doob, "Goebbels' Principles of Propaganda," *Public Opinion Quarterly* 14, no. 3 (1950): 428; Joseph Goebbels, "Aus Churchills Lügenfabrik," in *Die Zeit ohne Tagebücher von Joseph Goebbels*, Teil II, Band 3, *Januar-März* 1942 (Munich: Saur, 1994), 208–13. I thank Claudia Koonz, Nathan Stoltzfus, Sven Reichardt, Nikolai Wehrs, David Motadel, and Richard Evans for their comments and help regarding the history of this Goebbels misquotation.

2. See the excellent biography by Peter Longerich, *Goebbels: A Biography* (New York: Random House, 2015), 70–71, ix.

3. Ibid., 145, 696.

4. See Richard J. Evans, *The Coming of the Third Reich* (New York: Penguin Books, 2005), 397.

5. Adolf Hitler, *Mein Kampf* (New York: Mariner, 1999), 232.

6. Ernst Cassirer, *The Myth of the State* (New York: Doubleday, [1946] 1955), 354.

7. Benito Mussolini, *Opera omnia,* ed. Edoardo and Duilio Susmel (Florence: La Fenice, 1951–62), vol. 13, 45; vol. 7, 98: vol. 34, 117, 126.

8. Ibid, vol. 18, 457, 19, 49, 69.

9. See Benito Mussolini, *Scritti e discorsi di Benito Mussolini* (Milan: Hoepli, 1934), vol. 2, 345.

10. See Sophia Rosenfeld, *Democracy and Truth* (Philadelphia: University of Pennsylvania Press, 2019), 1.

11. See Robert Paxton, *The Anatomy of Fascism* (New York: Knopf, 2004), 16–17.

12. See Francisco Franco, *Palabras del caudillo: 19 abril 1937–31 de diciembre 1938* (Barcelona: Ediciones Fe, 1939), 149, 161, 276, 278.

13. See by Hannah Arendt, *Between Past and Future: Eight Exercises in Political Thought* (New York: Penguin, 2016), 228, 246, 249; and *The Origins of Totalitarianism* (New York: Meridian, 1959), 350.

14. See Hannah Arendt, *Eichmann in Jerusalem* (New York: Viking Press, 1965), 52.

15. On the Eichmann trial and the history of witnessing, see Carolyn J. Dean, *The Moral Witness: Trials and Testimony after Genocide* (Ithaca, NY: Cornell University Press, 2019).

16. See Arendt, *Eichmann in Jerusalem,* 252.

17. See Christopher R. Browning, *Collected Memories: Holocaust History and Postwar Testimony* (Madison: University of Wisconsin Press, 2003); David Cesarani, *Becoming Eichmann: Rethinking the Life, Crimes, and Trial of a "Desk Murderer"* (Cambridge, MA: Da Capo Press, 2006). For Arendt's contextual position vis-à-vis emerging Holocaust historiography, see Federico Finchelstein, "The Holocaust Canon: Rereading Raul Hilberg," *New German Critique* 96 (2006): 3–48. See also Richard Bernstein, *Hannah Arendt and the Jewish Question* (Cambridge, MA: MIT Press, 1996); Dan Stone, *History, Memory and Mass Atrocity: Essays on the Holocaust and Genocide* (London: Valentine Mitchell, 2006), 53–69.

18. Borges, *Obras completas* I, 580.

19. Arendt, *The Origins of Totalitarianism,* 474.

2. Truth and Mythology in the History of Fascism

1. Hannah Arendt, "The Seeds of a Fascist International," in *Essays in Understanding* 1930-1954, ed. Jerome Kohn (New York: Harcourt Brace, 1994), 147.

2. See Mabel Berezin, *Making the Fascist Self: The Political Culture of Interwar Italy* (Ithaca, NY: Cornell University Press, 1997), 198.

3. Federico Finchelstein, *From Fascism to Populism in History* (Oakland: University of California Press, 2017), 15, 37, 39, 41.

4. See by Jorge Luis Borges: "Thomas Carlyle," 35; "Thomas Carlyle: De los héroes," 37-41; and "Definición del Germanófilo," in *Obras completas* IV (Barcelona: Emecé, 1996), 442; "Ensayo de imparcialidad," *Sur* 61 (October 1939), 27.

5. On the liberal romantic tradition, see Pablo Piccato, *The Tyranny of Opinion* (Durham, NC: Duke University Press, 2010), 10, 11. See also Elías José Palti, *El momento romántico: Nación, historia y lenguajes políticos en la Argentina del siglo XIX* (Buenos Aires: Eudeba, 2009); Nadia Urbinati, *The Tyranny of the Moderns* (New Haven, CT: Yale University Press, 2015), 41, 55, 56.

6. See José Enrique Rodó, *Ariel* (Montevideo: Biblioteca Artigas, 1964), vol. 44. In *Ariel*, see especially 18, 19, 20; and in his writings on liberalism, see, e.g., 187, 188. See Leopoldo Lugones, *Política revolucionaria* (Buenos Aires: Anaconda, 1931), 17-19 and also 12-13, 15, 24-25, 29, 38. See also by Lugones: *Estudios helénicos* (Buenos Aires: Biblioteca Argentina de Buenas Ediciones Literarias, 1923), 18-21; *Nuevos estudios helénicos* (Buenos Aires: Babel, 1928), 23, 181.

7. Max Horkheimer, *Between Philosophy and Social Science* (Cambridge, MA: MIT Press, 1993), 278.

8. Ernst Cassirer, *The Myth of the State* (New York: Doubleday, [1946] 1955), 335.

9. Theodor W. Adorno, "Freudian Theory and the Pattern of Fascist Propaganda" (1951), in *Gesammelte Schriften* (Frankfurt: Suhrkamp, 1990), vol. 8, 429.

10. See Hannah Arendt, *The Origins of Totalitarianism* (New York: Meridian, 1959), 382-87.

3. Fascism Incarnate

1. Giussepe Bottai, "L'equivoco antifascista," *Critica Fascista*, April 1, 1924, 30. See also "L'espansione del fascismo," *Universalità Fascista* (February 1932): 96.

2. See Benedetto Croce, *Scritti e discorsi politici*, 1943–1947 (Bari: Laterza, 1963), I, 7; II, 46, 357. See also Renzo De Felice, *Interpretations of Fascism* (Cambridge, MA: Harvard University Press, 1977), 14–23; Pier Giorgio Zunino, *Interpretazione e memoria del fascismo: Gli anni del regime* (Rome: Laterza, 1991), 11–142.

3. See Dominick LaCapra, *History and Memory after Auschwitz* (Ithaca, NY: Cornell University Press, 1998), 104.

4. Corneliu Zelea Codreanu, *Manual del jefe* (Munich: Europa, 2004), 5.

5. Mussolini stated in 1929, "Gli osservatori stranieri notano che il popolo italiano parla poco, gestisce meno e sembra dominato da una sola volontà: è la politica del fascismo, la quale insegna che per divenire grandi secondo la màssima della filosofia del superuomo 'bisogna avere la gioia di obbedire a lungo e in una stessa direzione.'" See "Parla il duce del fascismo," *Il Giornale d'Italia*, September 15, 1929.

6. "Il mondo e nostro (terribile cosa!) perche que noi quasi inconsciamente ci siamo asunti di creare un mondo." Camillo Pellizzi, "Imperialismo o aristocrazia?," *Il Popolo d'Italia*, May 13, 1923. See also "Il comandamento del Duce," *Il Popolo d'Italia*, October 2, 1923; Nino Fattovich, "Sacra religio patriae (Divagazioni sul fascismo)," *Il Popolo d'Italia*, January 3, 1925; Antonio Pirazzoli, "Mussolini e il fascismo visti da lontano," *Il Popolo d'Italia*, March 15, 1925.

7. José Vasconcelos, cited in Pablo Yankelevich, "El exilio argentino de José Vasconcelos," *Revista Iberoamericana* 6, no. 24 (2006): 39.

8. On fascism and history, see Claudio Fogu, *The Historic Imaginary: Politics of History in Fascist Italy* (Toronto: University of Toronto Press, 2003); Fernando Esposito and Sven Reichardt, "Revolution and Eternity: Introductory Remarks on Fascist Temporalities," *Journal of Modern European History* 13 (2015): 24–43.

9. Volt, "Antistoria," *Critica Fascista*, January 15, 1927, 9–10.

10. The fascist intellectual Ardengo Soffici presented the fascist absolute as opposed to the theory of relativity proposed by a group of "German Jews whose capo is Einstein." See Ardengo Soffici, "Relativismo e politica," *Gerarchia* (January 1922): 34–35. See also a similar opposition by Mussolini in Sandra

Linguerri and Raffaella Simili, eds., *Einstein parla italiano: Itinerari e polemiche* (Bologna: Pendragon, 2008), 31.

11. See Tirso Molinari Morales, *El fascismo en el Perú* (Lima: Fondo Editorial de la Facultad de Ciencias Sociales, 2006), 186.

12. See the insightful analysis of Markus Daechsel, "Scientism and Its Discontents: The Indo-Muslim 'Fascism' of Inayatullah Khan al-Mashriqi," *Modern Intellectual History* 3, no. 3 (2006): 462, 463.

13. See James P. Jankowski, "The Egyptian Blue Shirts and the Egyptian Wafd, 1935–1938," *Middle Eastern Studies* 6, no. 1 (January 1970): 87; Reto Hofmann, *The Fascist Effect: Japan and Italy, 1915–1952* (Ithaca, NY: Cornell University Press, 2015), 81–83.

14. See Hofmann, *The Fascist Effect*, 86; see also Harry Harootunian's review of the book *Hirohito Redux—Hirohito and the Making of Modern Japan* by Herbert P. Bix in *Critical Asian Studies* 33, no. 4 (2001): 609–36. I would like to thank Reto Hofmann for his comments regarding these dimensions of Japanese fascism.

15. See Israel Gershoni and James Jankowski, *Confronting Fascism in Egypt: Dictatorship versus Democracy in the 1930s* (Stanford, CA: Stanford University Press, 2009), 236.

4. Enemies of the Truth?

1. Adolf Hitler, *Mein Kampf* (New York: Mariner, 1999), 65; original emphasis.

2. José Vasconcelos, "Contra los planes ocultos, la luz de la verdad," *Timón*, no. 13 (1940). Reprinted in Itzhak M. Bar-Lewaw, ed., *La Revista "Timón" y José Vasconcelos* (Mexico City: Edimex, 1971), 143–44.

3. Pablo Yankelevich, "El exilio argentino de José Vasconcelos," *Revista Iberoamericana* 6, no. 24 (2006): 37. On Vasconcelos, see also Claude Fell, *José Vasconcelos: Los años del águila (1920–1925)* (Mexico City: Universidad Nacional Autónoma de México, 1989). On Mexican fascism, see also Jean Meyer, *El sinarquismo: ¿Un fascismo mexicano? 1937–1947* (Mexico City: Joaquín Mortiz, 1979).

4. See Fernando de Euzcadi, "Judaismo vs. Catolicismo," *Timón*, no. 12 (1940). Reprinted in Bar-Lewaw, *La Revista "Timón" y José Vasconcelos*, 222–25.

5. Hitler, *Mein Kampf*, 318; see also 324.

6. On Argentine clerico-fascism, see Federico Finchelstein, *Transatlantic Fascism: Ideology, Violence, and the Sacred in Argentina and Italy*, 1919–1945 (Durham, NC: Duke University Press, 2010).

7. Julio Meinvielle, *El judío* (Buenos Aires: Antídoto, 1936), 11; Virgilio Filippo, *Los judíos: Juicio histórico científico que el autor no pudo transmitir por L. R. S Radio París* (Buenos Aires: Tor, 1939), 111.

8. Virgilio Filippo, *Conferencias radiotelefónicas* (Buenos Aires: Tor, 1936), 215. These European stereotypes have been analyzed by such authors as George L. Mosse and Sander Gilman. See George L. Mosse, *Nationalism and Sexuality* (New York: Howard Fertig, 1985); George L. Mosse, *The Image of Man: The Creation of Modern Masculinity* (Oxford: Oxford University Press, 1996); Sander Gilman, *The Jew's Body* (New York: Routledge, 1991).

9. See Simon Levis Sullam, *L'archivio antiebraico: Il linguaggio dell' antisemitismo moderno* (Rome: Laterza, 2008). On anti-Semitism as a cultural code, see Shulamit Volkov, "Anti-Semitism as a Cultural Code: Reflections on the History and Historiography of Anti-Semitism in Imperial Germany," *Yearbook of the Leo Baeck Institute* 23 (1978): 25–46. On anti-Semitism, see also Paul Hanebrink, *A Specter Haunting Europe: The Myth of Judeo-Bolshevism* (Cambridge, MA: Harvard University Press, 2018). On anti-Judaism, see David Nirenberg, *Anti-Judaism: The Western Tradition* (New York: Norton, 2013).

10. See "Los judíos en la República Argentina: Breve reseña de las sucesivas invasiones," *Acción Antijudía Argentina* 13 (1939): 1; Virgilio Filippo, *¿Quiénes tienen las manos limpias? Estudios sociológicos* (Buenos Aires: Tor, 1939), 127.

11. Filippo, *Los judíos*, 44, 45, 49.

12. As the historian of anti-Semitism Michele Battini explains, "Anti-Semitic propaganda states a fact that never happened and falsifies the evidence that would demolish it, yet it tells the truth about its own persecutory intentions because its authors were certain that they were able to deceive public opinion and even those who did not believe it." The power to distinguish between true and false was reserved for those who could lie in plain sight but also explicitly reveal their destructive intentions. Michele Battini, *Socialism of Fools: Capitalism and Modern Anti-Semitism* (New York: Columbia University Press, 2016), 9.

13. See Valeria Galimi, *Sotto gli occhi di tutti: La società italiana e le persecuzioni contro gli ebrei* (Florence: Le Monnier, 2018).

14. See Bruno Jacovella, "El judío es el enemigo del pueblo cristiano," *Crisol,* October 13, 1936; *Clarinada* (June 1942): 31.

15. Theodor W. Adorno, *Minima Moralia* (New York: Verso, 2005), 108.

16. Enzo Traverso, *The Origins of Nazi Violence* (New York: New Press, 2003), xx.

17. See all these references in Federico Finchelstein, *From Fascism to Populism in History* (Oakland: University of California Press, 2017), 73–81.

18. Jorge González von Marées, *El mal de Chile (sus causas y sus remedios)* (Santiago: Talleres gráficos "Portales," 1940), 53.

19. Corneliu Zelea Codreanu, *Manual del jefe* (Munich: Europa, 2004), 130–31.

5. Truth and Power

1. "Il nostro orgoglio e la nostra sicurezza di grande Nazione. Tra le incertezze di altri Popoli noi abbiamo: un regime saldo. . . . La parola precisa e decisa del Duce, il quale vede, prevede e provvede, ed ha sempre ragione." Archivo del Ministerio de Relaciones Exteriores y Culto, Argentina, División Política, Caja 2386, Italia, Exp. 1, Año 1933, n. 39, R.E. 1/33, *Giornale d'Italia,* March 11, 1933; "Mussolini ha sempre ragione," *Universalità Fascista* (July-August 1939): 423; "Mussolini dittatore del partito," *Critica Fascista,* September 15, 1926, 344.

2. "Nuestras lecturas," *El Fascio* (Madrid), March 16, 1933, 13.

3. See Federico Finchelstein, *El mito del fascismo: De Freud a Borges* (Buenos Aires: Capital Intelectual, 2015).

4. See Theodor W. Adorno, "Freudian Theory and the Pattern of Fascist Propaganda" (1951), in *Gesammelte Schriften* (Frankfurt: Suhrkamp, 1990), vol. 8, 408–33; Sigmund Freud, *Group Psychology and the Analysis of the Ego* (London: Hogarth Press, 1940), 115.

5. Finchelstein, *El mito del fascismo,* 43–77.

6. Hannah Arendt, *The Origins of Totalitarianism* (New York: Meridian, 1959), 349.

7. See Alfredo Rocco, "Per la cooperazione intellettuale dei popoli," *Critica Fascista,* March 1, 1926, 52. See also Archivio Centrale dello Stato, Rome, Italy, MRF B 58 F 129 "CANZONI FASCISTE," Cart. 1, "Per te, o Mussolini!"; Cart. 3, "Saluto al Duce"; and in the same archival folder but not included in the

cartelle, "Inno al fondatore dell' impero"; Arturo Foà, "Fascismo e classicismo," *Il Popolo d'Italia,* May 18, 1928; Giuseppe Bottai, "Ritratto di Demostene," *Critica Fascista,* March 1, 1926, 53. For this notion of heroism and truth in Argentine fascism, see Federico Ibarguren, *Rosas y la tradición hispanoamericana* (Buenos Aires: n.p., 1942), 4. For Hitler, see, e.g., the symptomatic considerations of the Argentine fascist Julio Irazusta, "La personalidad de Hitler," *Nuevo Orden,* May 14, 1941; of the Spanish fascist Ramón Serrano Suñer, in Archivo del Ministerio de Relaciones Exteriores y Culto, Argentina, División Política, mueble 7, casilla 22, *Guerra Europea,* exp. 258, año 1940; and Archivo del Ministerio de Relaciones Exteriores y Culto, Argentina, Caja 14, España, exp. 1, 1945.

8. Adolf Hitler, *Speeches and Proclamations,* 1932–1945, ed. Max Domarus (London: Tauris, 1990), vol. 1, 420.

9. Ernesto Giménez Caballero, *La nueva catolicidad: Teoría general sobre el fascismo en Europa* (Madrid: La Gazeta Literaria, 1933), 128–29, 131–32.

10. See Leopoldo Lugones, "El único candidato," in *Escritos políticos,* ed. María Pía López and Guillermo Korn (Buenos Aires: Losada, 2011), 320. On the fascist notion of liberalism as presenting half-truths or even lies, see José María Pemán, "Perfiles de la nueva barbarie," *Acción Española,* January 1, 1932, 131–41.

11. José Millán Astray, *Franco el caudillo* (Salamanca: M. Quero y Simón Editor, 1939), cited in Antonio Cazorla, *Franco, biografía del mito* (Madrid: Alianza, 2015), 105. On other Spanish fascist myths of the leader, see Joan Maria Thomàs, *José Antonio Primo de Rivera: The Reality and Myth of a Spanish Fascist Leader* (New York: Berghahn Books, 2019).

12. Corneliu Zelea Codreanu, *Manual del jefe* (Munich: Europa, 2004), 182.

13. Jacques Derrida, *Historia de la mentira: Prolegómenos* (Buenos Aires: Universidad de Buenos Aires, Facultad de Filosofía y Letras Press, 1995), 36, 38, 43.

14. Dominick LaCapra, *Writing History, Writing Trauma* (Baltimore: Johns Hopkins University Press, 2001), 49, 50.

15. See Hans Blumenberg, *The Legitimacy of the Modern Age* (Cambridge, MA: MIT Press, 1983); Derrida, *Historia de la mentira,* 25.

16. On Nazi redemptive anti-Semitism, see Saul Friedlander, *Nazi Germany and the Jews: The Tears of Persecution,* 1933–1939 (New York: HarperCol-

lins, 1997); Enzo Traverso, *The Origins of Nazi Violence* (New York: New Press, 2003). On fascism and political religion, see Emilio Gentile, *Le religioni della politica: Fra democrazie e totalitarismi* (Rome: Laterza, 2001). On Heiddeger, Nazism, and anti-Semitism, see Donatella Di Cesare, *Heidegger and the Jews: The Black Notebooks* (Cambridge: Polity, 2018).

17. Ramiro de Maeztu, "¿No hay hombres?," *ABC*, March 26, 1936.

18. They claimed that de Maeztu had given "his life for the Truth." See "Vox clamantis in deserto," *Acción Española* (March 1937): 6-7. See also "Tre Gennaio," *Augustea* (1943): 35.

19. See Lloyd E. Eastman, "Fascism in Kuomintang China: The Blue Shirts," *China Quarterly*, no. 49 (January–March 1972): 9. On fascism in China, see also Maggie Clinton, *Revolutionary Nativism: Fascism and Culture, 1925-1937* (Durham, NC: Duke University Press, 2017); Brian Tsui, *China's Conservative Revolution: The Quest for a New Order, 1927-1949* (Cambridge: Cambridge University Press, 2018).

20. Alfred Rosenberg, *The Myth of the Twentieth Century* (Torrance, CA: Noontide Press, 1982), 61-62.

21. Kevin Passmore, *Fascism: A Very Short Introduction* (Oxford: Oxford Univeristy Press, 2014), 86. On Romanian fascism, see Constantin Iordachi, "God's Chosen Warriors: Romantic Palingenesis, Militarism and Fascism in Modern Romania," in *Comparative Fascist Studies: New Perspectives*, ed. Constantin Iordachi (London: Routledge, 2009), 316-57.

22. Julius Evola, *Il mito del sangue* (Milan: Hoepli, 1937). On Italian anti-Semitism, see Simon Levis Sullam, *The Italian Executioners: The Genocide of the Jews of Italy* (Princeton, NJ: Princeton University Press, 2018); Valeria Galimi, *Sotto gli occhi di tutti* (Florence: Le Monnier, 2018); Marie Anne Matard-Bonucci, *L'Italia fascista e la persecuzione degli ebrei* (Bologna: Il Mulino, 2008).

23. See Carl Schmitt, "El fuhrer defiende el derecho" (1934), in *Carl Schmitt, teólogo de la política*, ed. Héctor Orestes Aguilar (Mexico City: Fondo de Cultura Económica, 2001), 114-18.

24. Ibid.; see also Ingo Müller, *Hitler's Justice: The Courts of the Third Reich* (Cambridge, MA: Harvard University Press, 1991), 70-79. On Schmitt's receptivity to fascism, see the compelling argument in Jean Cohen and Andrew Arato, *Civil Society and Political Theory* (Cambridge, MA: MIT Press, 1992), 240. On the contemporary need to study Schmitt, see Andreas Kalyvas, *Democracy and the Politics of the Extraordinary: Max Weber, Carl Schmitt, and Hannah*

Arendt (Cambridge: Cambridge University Press, 2008), esp. 80–67. Nadia Urbinati has cogently noted Schmitt's participation in a long antidemocratic tradition that perceives democracy as the manipulation of truth. See Nadia Urbinati, *Democracy Disfigured: Opinion, Truth, and the People* (Cambridge, MA: Harvard University Press, 2014), 88.

25. Antonio Gramsci, *Gli intellettuali* (Rome: Editori Riuniti, 1979), 93.

26. Hans Frank, cited in Hannah Arendt, *Eichmann in Jerusalem* (New York: Viking Press, 1965), 136. On Arendt's interpretation of this imperative in Eichmann, see 137, 148, 149.

27. Gustavo Barroso, *Reflexões de um bode* (Rio de Janeiro: Gráf. Educadora Limitada, 1937), 169, 177, 178.

28. Plínio Salgado, *Palavra nova dos tempos novos* (Rio de Janeiro: Olympio, 1936), 114–15. On Salgado and Brazilian fascism, see Leandro Pereira Gonçalves, *Plínio Salgado: Um Católico integralista entre Portugal e o Brasil (1895–1975)* (Rio de Janeiro: FGV Editora, 2018).

29. Silvio Villegas, *No hay enemigos a la derecha* (Manizales: Arturo Zapata, 1937), 43, 46, 50, 57, 78. See also Leopoldo Lugones, "Una página de estética," *Repertorio Americano*, October 27, 1924, 113–15.

30. Salgado, *Palavra nova dos tempos novos*, 114–15. See also Plínio Salgado, *O doutrina do sigma* (Rio de Janeiro: Schmidt, 1937), 168.

6. Revelations

1. "Il convegno di mistica fascista," *Il Legionario*, March 1, 1940, 4, 5.

2. Ivan, "Tra i libri," *Gerarchia* (August 1939). See also Titta Madia, "'Duce' Biografia della parola," *Gerarchia* (1937): 382. As the fascist Telesio Interlandi told Mussolini in a private letter, the Duce's words could not be truly understood by reading them for they transcended their explicit meaning. See Letter to Mussolini from Telesio Interlandi, Archivio Centrale dello Stato, Rome, Italy, Ministero della Cultura Popolare, D. G. Serv. Propaganda, Gabinetto B. 43 260.2 (1941).

3. Curzio Malaparte, "Botta e risposta," *Critica Fascista*, November 15, 1926, 419–20.

4. Archivio Centrale dello Stato, Rome, Italy, MRF B 58 F 129 "CANZONI FASCISTE," Cart. 1, "Dux" and "L'Aquila legionaria."

5. Federico Forni, "Appunti sulla dottrina," *Gerarchia* (1939): 459-60. On this, see also by the Spanish fascist Víctor Pradera, "Los falsos dogmas," *Acción Española* (1932): 113-22.

6. Alfred Rosenberg, *The Myth of the Twentieth Century* (Torrance, CA: Noontide Press, 1982), 432.

7. Plínio Salgado, *Palavra nova dos tempos novos* (Rio de Janeiro: Olympio, 1936), 115. See also Plínio Salgado, *O doutrina do sigma* (Rio de Janeiro: Schmidt, 1937), 168.

8. See Partito Nazionale Fascista, *Foglio d'Ordini*, no. 147, November 18, 1935, Archivio Centrale dello Stato, Rome, Italy, Archivi Fascisti, Segreteria Particolare del Duce, Cart. riservato, B 31 F Gran Consiglio SF 13 1935. On justice and fighting, see also Angelo Tarchi, "Perché combattiamo," *Repubblica Sociale* (1945): 4, 11; and *La Verità* (Venice: Erre, 1944), 19, 25.

9. Alexandre Koyré, "The Political Function of the Modern Lie," *Contemporary Jewish Record* 8 (1945): 290-300. See also Jacques Derrida, *Historia de la mentira: Prolegómenos* (Buenos Aires: Universidad de Buenos Aires, Facultad de Filosofía y Letras Press, 1995), 43, 47-48; and Hannah Arendt, "Truth and Politics," *New Yorker*, February 25, 1967.

10. Leopoldo Lugones, "Rehallazgo del país," *La Nación*, November 8, 1936.

11. See Ramiro de Maeztu, "El valor de la Hispanidad," *Acción Española* (1932): 561-71; and "El valor de la Hispanidad II," *Acción Española* (1932): 1-11.

12. Gustavo Barroso, *O integralismo e o mundo* (Rio de Janeiro: Civilização Brasileira, 1936), 16, 17.

13. Ibid., 145.

14. Salgado, *Palavra nova dos tempos novos*, 116-17.

15. Ibid.

16. Corneliu Zelea Codreanu, *Manual del jefe* (Munich: Europa, 2004), 151-52.

17. Sir Oswald Mosley, 10 *Points of Fascism* (London: B.U.F., 1933), 2-3.

18. Derrida cogently criticizes this idea that truth can be owned in politics, but both Arendt and Koyré seem to insist on the nonpolitical nature of their insights. For a converging criticism of Arendt, see Ágnes Heller, *Solo se sono libera* (Rome: Castelvecchi, 2014), 16.

19. See Jorge Luis Borges, "De la dirección de Proa," in Jorge Luis Borges, *Textos recobrados (1931-1955)* (Barcelona: Emecé, 1997), vol. 1, 207-8; Federico

Finchelstein, *El mito del fascismo: De Freud a Borges* (Buenos Aires: Capital Intelectual, 2015).

20. See Jorge Luis Borges, "El propósito de Zarathustra," in Borges, *Textos recobrados*, vol. 2, 211–18; *The Diary of Sigmund Freud, 1929–1939*, ed. Michael Molnar (New York: Maxwell Macmillan, 1992), 149.

21. See Omero Valle, "Dell' intelligenza fascista," *Gerarchia* (1939): 703.

22. See Italo Calvino, "Il Duce's Portraits," *New Yorker*, January 6, 2003.

23. José Carlos Mariátegui, *Obra política* (Mexico City: Era, 1979), 122, 124, 137.

24. Theodor W. Adorno, "Anti-Semitism and Fascist Propaganda" (1946), in *Gesammelte Schriften* (Frankfurt: Suhrkamp, 1990), vol. 8, 398, 403.

25. See Archivio Centrale dello Stato, Rome, Italy, Archivi Fascisti, Segreteria Particolare del Duce, Carteggio riservato, B1 F 2 SF 9 GENTILE GIOVANNI; Giovanni Gentile, "La legge del gran consiglio," *Educazione Fascista* (September 1928). See also Luigi Chiarini, "Coscienza imperiale," *Critica Fascista*, June 15, 1928, 235; Enzo Capaldo, "Attualità della vigilia nella formazione della coscienza fascista," *Critica Fascista*, January 1, 1934, 20.

7. The Fascist Unconscious

1. A.M., "I segni del tempo," *Il Popolo d'Italia*, January 1, 1928. See also "Senso dell' eterno in Mussolini," *La Repubblica Fascista*, December 22, 1944, 1.

2. Adolf Hitler, *Mein Kampf* (Boston: Mariner, 2001), 510.

3. Ibid., 509–12.

4. Zeev Sternhell, *The Anti-Enlightenment Tradition* (New Haven, CT: Yale University Press, 2010), 318, 329, 328.

5. Michele Bianchi, "Il concetto di rappresentanza nello Stato fascista," *Il Giornale d'Italia*, November 27, 1929, 1.

6. Edgardo Sulis, ed., *Mussolini contro il mito di demos* (Milan: Hoepli, 1942) 71, 72. See also Gustavo Barroso, "Procurador dos descaminhos," *A Offensiva*, April 13, 1935; and the British fascist leader Sir Oswald Mosley, *Fascism: 100 Questions Asked and Answered* (London: B.U.F., 1936), 15. On the history of the concept of sovereignty, see Dieter Grimm, *Sovereignty: The Origins and Future of a Political and Legal Concept* (New York: Columbia University Press, 2015).

7. See Benito Mussolini, *Scritti e discorsi di Benito Mussolini* (Milan: Hoepli, 1934), vol. 3, 108; Simonetta Falasca-Zamponi, *Fascist Spectacle: The*

Aesthetics of Power in Mussolini's Italy (Berkeley: University of California Press, 1997), 258.

8. Plínio Salgado, *A doutrina do sigma* (Rio de Janeiro: Schmidt, 1937), 21; Alfonso de Laferrere, *Literatura y política* (Buenos Aires: Manuel Gleizer, 1928), 128; Silvio Villegas, *No hay enemigos a la derecha* (Manizales: Arturo Zapata, 1937), 224. On Mussolini and Sorel, see Falasca-Zamponi, *Fascist Spectacle*, 213; Emil Ludwig, *Colloqui con Mussolini* (Milan: Mondadori, 1932), 124; Benito Mussolini, *Opera omnia*, ed. Edoardo and Duilio Susmel (Florence: La Fenice, 1951–62), vol. 20, 123. On Nazism and moral rebirth, see Claudia Koonz, *The Nazi Conscience* (Cambride, MA: Belknap Press of Harvard University Press, 2003), 31 and 33, 75.

9. See Mussolini, *Scritti e discorsi di Benito Mussolini*, vol. 5, 322.

10. Roberto Pavese, "Filosofia e religione nel momento presente," *Gerarchia* (November (1936): 761. See also Cesare Colliva, "Impero fascista," *Meridiani* (March–April 1936).

11. See Camillo Pellizzi, "Pensiero fascista," *Il Popolo d'Italia*, April 5, 1925. See also Alessandro Pavolini, "La funzione del partito," *Critica Fascista*, July 1, 1926, 171.

12. See "Il messaggio del Duce," *Il Giornale d'Italia*, October 27, 1935; Mussolini, *Opera omnia*, vol. 32, 105; Sulis, *Mussolini contro il mito di demos*, 49. See also Francesco Maria Barracu, *La voce della patria* (Venice: Erre, 1944), 15, 18. For the songs "Inno a Mussolini" and "Inno dedicato agli Eroi della Rivoluzione Fascista," see Archivio Centrale dello Stato, Rome, Italy, MRF B 58 F 129 "CANZONI FASCISTE," Cart. 1 and Cart. 3.

13. Camillo Pellizzi, "Educazione fascista," *Il Popolo d'Italia*, February 10, 1928.

14. Volt, "L'imperialismo economico," *Il Popolo d'Italia*, 1923. See also Nardo Naldoni, "La guerra," *Meridiani* (June 1936): 2.3.

15. See Federico Finchelstein, "On Fascist Ideology," *Constellations* 15 (2008): 320–31. On fascism, see also the following important works: Zeev Sternhell, *Ni droite ni gauche: L'idéologie fasciste en France* (Paris: Gallimard, 2012); Ruth Ben-Ghiat, *Fascist Modernities* (Berkeley: University of California Press, 2001); Geoff Eley, *Nazism as Fascism: Violence, Ideology and the Ground of Consent in Germany* (London: Routledge, 2013); António Costa Pinto, *The Nature of Fascism Revisited* (Boulder, CO: Social Science Monographs, 2012); Angelo Ventrone, *La seduzione totalitaria: Guerra, modernità, violenza politica: 1914–1918* (Rome: Donzelli, 2003); Emilio Gentile, *Fascismo: Storia e interpretazione* (Rome: Laterza, 2002); Giulia Albanese, "Brutalizzazione e violenza

alle origini del fascismo," *Studi Storici* 1 (2014): 3–14; Sandra Deutsch, *Las Derechas: The Extreme Right in Argentina, Brazil, and Chile* 1890–1939 (Stanford, CA: Stanford University Press, 1999); Joan Maria Thomàs, *Los fascismos españoles* (Barcelona: Ariel, 2019).

16. See Benito Mussolini, "Vivere pericolosamente" (1924), in Mussolini, *Opera omnia*, vol. 21, 40, 41. See also by Ernesto Giménez Caballero, "Tre fasi del generale Franco," *Gerarchia* (1937): 153; and *Genio de España* (Madrid: La Gaceta Literaria, 1932), 134, 318.

17. Romans 3:4; 1 John 2:22; John 8:43–45 (NRSV).

18. Leonardo Castellani, *Las canciones de Militis: Seis ensayos y tres cartas* (Buenos Aires: Ediciones Dictio, 1973), 61.

19. See Ernesto Giménez Caballero, *Genio de España: Exaltaciones a una resurrección nacional y del mundo* (Zaragoza: Ediciones Jerarquía, 1938), 211; and his *Casticismo, nacionalismo y vanguardia: Antología, 1927–1935* (Madrid: Fundación Santander Central Hispano, 2005), 73, 105, 172.

20. See Giménez Caballero, *Casticismo, nacionalismo y vanguardia*, 73, 102, 103, 129, 160, 183, 241–42.

8. Fascism against Psychoanalysis

1. Carlos Meneses, *Cartas de juventud de J. L. Borges (1921–1922)* (Madrid: Orígenes, 1987), 15.

2. See Leopoldo Lugones, "La formación del ciudadano," *La Nación*, February 13, 1938.

3. Albérico S. Lagomarsino, *La cuestión judía: Su estudio analítico y crítico* (Buenos Aires: n.p., 1936), 84–87.

4. Virgilio Filippo, *Los judíos: Juicio histórico científico que el autor no pudo transmitir por L. R. S. Radio Paris* (Buenos Aires: Tor, 1939), 217.

5. Freud actually had cancer of the jaw, not the tongue. See Leonardo Castellani, *Freud en cifra* (Buenos Aires: Cruz y Fierro, 1966), 11. Many fascists, including Castellani, compared Vienna to Buenos Aires and claimed that both cities were "monstrously" overwhelmed by the Jews. See Degreff, *Esperanza de Israel* (Buenos Aires: F. A. Colombo, 1938), 51. For them, both cities faced a pollutant from a lower world that was a combination of both modern and ancient threats to Christianity and its foremost creation, "the white race." See Vezzetti's suggestive analysis of Castellani in his introduction to Hugo Vezzetti, ed.,

Freud en Buenos Aires, 1910–1939 (Buenos Aires: Puntosur, 1989), 71–72; Leonardo Castellani, "Sigmund Freud (1856–1939)," *La Nación*, October 8, 1939, sec. 2, 1–2.

6. Adolf Hitler, *Mein Kampf* (New York: Mariner, 1999), 325.

7. Gustavo Franceschi, "Como se prepara una revolución," *Criterio*, September 14, 1933, 30; "Una Europa sin judíos," *Bandera Argentina*, February 1, 1941, 1.

8. Julio Meinvielle, "Catolicismo y nacionalismo," *El Pueblo*, October 18, 1936, 3.

9. Julio Meinvielle, *Entre la Iglesia y el Reich* (Buenos Aires: Adsum, 1937), 68.

10. Fernando de Euzcadi, "Judaismo vs. Catolicismo," *Timón*, no. 12 (1940). Reprinted in Itzhak M. Bar-Lewaw, ed., *La Revista "Timón" y José Vasconcelos* (Mexico City: Edimex, 1971), 225.

11. Ibid., 222–25.

12. Filippo, *Los judíos*, 197.

13. Virgilio Filippo, *El reinado de Satanás: Conferencias irradiadas dominicalmente a las 13 horas desde L. R. 8, Radio París de Bs. As.* (Buenos Aires: Tor, 1937), vol. 2, 109.

14. On fascism and psychoanalysis in Italy, see Piero Meldini, *Mussolini contro Freud: La psicoanalisi nella pubblicistica fascista* (Florence: Guaraldi, 1976); Michel David, *La psicoanalisi nella cultura italiana* (Turin: Boringhieri, 1966); Mauro Pasqualini, "Origin, Rise, and Destruction of a Psychoanalytic Culture in Fascist Italy, 1922–1938," in *Psychoanalysis and Politics*, ed. Joy Damousi and Mariano Plotkin (New York: Oxford University Press, 2012); Roberto Zapperi, *Freud e Mussolini: La psicoanalisi in Italia durante il regime fascista* (Milan: Franco Angeli, 2013); Maddalena Carli, "Saluti da Vienna, o duce," *Il Manifesto*, September 25, 2014. For psychoanalysis and antifascism, see Eli Zaretsky, *Secrets of the Soul: A Social and Cultural History of Psychoanalysis* (New York: Knopf, 2004), 244–45.

15. See Fermi, "Psicanalisi e psicosintesi," *Gerarchia* (1935): 817; Roberto Suster, "Elementi di psicologia germanica," *Critica Fascista*, February 1934, 55; "Psicoanalisi e castità," *La Difesa della Razza*, November 20, 1941, 31.

16. Benito Mussolini, "Labirinto comunista," in Benito Mussolini, *Opera omnia*, ed. Edoardo and Duilio Susmel (Florence: La Fenice, 1951–62), vol. 26, 11–12.

17. Castellani argued that "it is known that a true Freudian will not denounce it; Freudianism is a kind of religion"; Juan Palmetta, "Fe de erratas: Freud. I. La Vida: Freudiana del niño," *Criterio*, October 5, 1939, 107.

18. Plínio Salgado, *O doutrina do sigma* (Rio de Janeiro: Schmidt, 1937), 157, 158.

19. See Ellevi, "Tra i libri," *Gerarchia* (1941): 57. See also Lidio Cipriani, "Quale la vera responsabile: Albione o Israele?," *Gerarchia* (1940): 519; Ellevi, "La democracia, secolo d'oro dell'ebraismo," *Gerarchia* (1938): 806; Julius Evola, *Sintesi di Dottrina della Razza* (Milan: Hoepli, 1941), 148–49; Ernesto Pesci, *Lotta e destino di razza* (Alterocca: Terni, 1939).

20. Was this dimension exclusive to fascists? As Adorno explained this situation in 1944, nobody or nothing (not even Freudian theory and certainly not capitalist society) was exempted from this pattern in which the subject becomes "untruth." To be sure, Adorno noted, in Freud's thinking, a tension existed between the emancipation and the normalization of the subject in the bourgeois world. But, notably, Adorno warned that psychoanalysis also ran the risk of becoming a "follow my leader behavior" that was connected to a situation in which "truth is abandoned to relativity and people to power." If the "terror against the abyss of the self" was fully normalized and the self was annulled by means of formulas, psychoanalysis also risked becoming a normalizing response to the total alienation of bourgeois society. See Theodor W. Adorno, *Minima Moralia* (New York: Verso, 2005), 60–66.

21. See Giuseppe Maggiore, "Logica e moralità del razzismo," *La Difesa della Razza*, September 5, 1938, 32; Alfonso Petrucci, "Morte dell'ultimo illusionista," *La Difesa della Razza*, November 20, 1941, 27, 28, 31.

22. Domenico Rende, "Il pansessualismo di Freud," *La Difesa della Razza*, October 5, 1938, 43, 45.

23. See Saul Friedlander, *Nazi Germany and the Jews: The Tears of Persecution, 1933–1939* (New York: HarperCollins, 1997), 172. See also Sander Gilman, *Freud, Race, and Gender* (Princeton, NJ: Princeton University Press, 1993), 31.

24. On this theme, see especially the pioneering work of Meldini, *Mussolini contro Freud*. On Italian "volontarismo," see, e.g., the symptomatic article by Antonio Monti, "Contributo ad una sintesi storica del volontarismo," *Gerarchia* (1936): 389–92. See also Umberto Mascia, "Il volontarismo italiano da Roma al fascismo," *Gerarchia* (1930): 1030–34.

25. See Friedlander, *Nazi Germany and the Jews*, 191; see also Enzo Traverso, *The Origins of Nazi Violence* (New York: New Press, 2003), 95.

26. See Georges Sorel, *Reflections on Violence* (New York: Peter Smith, 1941), 137, 167.

9. Democracy and Dictatorship

1. Adolf Hitler, *Mein Kampf* (New York: Mariner, 1999), 316, 325-27.

2. Ugo D'Andrea, "Teoria e pratica della reazione politica," *Critica Fascista*, February 1, 1925, 41.

3. See Joseph Fronczak, "The Fascist Game: Transnational Political Transmission and the Genesis of the U.S. Modern Right," *Journal of American History* 105, no. 3 (December 2018): 586; Benjamin Zachariah, "A Voluntary Gleichschaltung? Indian Perspectives Towards a Non-Eurocentric Understanding of Fascism," *Transcultural Studies* 2 (2014): 82.

4. Maria Hsia Chang, *The Chinese Blue Shirts Society* (Berkeley, CA: Institute of East Asian Studies, 1985), 27, 19-20.

5. "El fascismo y la democracia," *El Fascio* (Madrid), March 16, 1933, 5.

6. See José Vasconcelos, "Otro fantasma: El nazismo en la América española," *Timón*, no. 11 (1940); and Editorial, *Timón*, no. 15 (1940). Both articles are reprinted in Itzhak M. Bar-Lewaw, ed., *La Revista "Timón" y José Vasconcelos* (Mexico City: Edimex, 1971), 138-39 and 102, respectively.

7. See Raul Ferrero, *Marxismo y nacionalismo: Estado nacional corporativo* (Lima: Editorial Lumen, 1937), 125, 187; R. Havard de la Montagne, "Démocratie politique et démocratie sociale," *Action française*, May 14, 1941, 1.

8. Leopoldo Lugones, *El estado equitativo (Ensayo sobre la realidad Argentina)* (Buenos Aires: La Editora Argentina, 1932), 11.

9. Leopoldo Lugones, *Política revolucionaria* (Buenos Aires: Anaconda, 1931), 52, 53, 65-66; Lugones, *El estado equitativo*, 9, 11.

10. Leopoldo Lugones, "Un voto en blanco," *La Nación*, December 3, 1922. See also Leopoldo Lugones, *Escritos políticos* (Buenos Aires: Losada, 2009), 191.

11. Leopoldo Lugones, "Ante una nueva perspectiva del gobierno del mundo," *La Fronda*, January 16, 1933, 7.

12. For some interesting Argentine examples, see Archivo General de la Nación [hereafter AGN], Archivo Agustín P. Justo, Caja 36, doc. 277, Reacción

1 quincena junio 1935, no. 1, "La Legión cívica argentina"; Guido Glave, *Economía dirigida de la democracia corporativa argentina* (Buenos Aires: Imprenta L. L. Gotelli, 1936), 7, 25, 30, 135-36; AGN, Archivo Agustín P. Justo, Caja 104, doc. 151, February 28, 1942.

13. AGN, Archivo Agustín P. Justo, Caja 49, doc. 29, Nueva Idea año 1, no. 1, 19 enero 1935; Héctor Bernardo, *El régimen corporativo y el mundo actual* (Buenos Aires: Adsum, 1943), 52-54.

14. Charles Maier, *Recasting Bourgeois Europe* (Princeton, NJ: Princeton University Press, 1988).

15. As the historian António Costa Pinto observes, "Powerful processes of institutional transfers were a hallmark of interwar dictatorships. . . . Corporatism was at the forefront of this process, both as a new form of organized interest representation and as an authoritarian alternative to parliamentary democracy. The diffusion of political and social corporatism, which with the single party are hallmarks of the institutional transfers among European dictatorships, challenges some rigid dichotomous interpretations of interwar fascism." António Costa Pinto, *The Nature of Fascism Revisited* (New York: SSM— Columbia University Press, 2012), xix. See also his *Latin American Dictatorships in the Era of Fascism* (London: Routledge, 2020).

16. See Antonio Costa Pinto and Federico Finchelstein, ed., *Authoritarian Intellectuals and Corporatism in Europe and Latin America* (London: Routledge, 2019). See also António Costa Pinto, "Fascism, Corporatism and the Crafting of Authoritarian Institutions in Interwar European Dictatorships," in *Rethinking Fascism and Dictatorship in Europe*, ed. António Costa Pinto and Aristotle A Kallis (Basingstoke: Palgrave Macmillan, 2014), 87; Matteo Passetti, "Neither Bluff nor Revolution: The Corporations and the Consolidation of the Fascist Regime (1925-1926)," in *In the Society of Fascists: Acclamation, Acquiescence, and Agency in Mussolini's Italy*, ed. Giulia Albanese and Roberta Pergher (Basingstoke: Palgrave Macmillan, 2012); Alessio Gagliardi, *Il corporativismo fascista* (Rome: Laterza, 2010); Philip Morgan, "Corporatism and the Economic Order," in *The Oxford Handbook of Fascism*, ed. R. J. B. Bosworth (Oxford: Oxford University Press, 2019), 150-65; Fabio Gentile, "O estado corporativo fascista e sua apropriação na era Vargas," in *Ditaduras—a desmesura do poder*, ed. Nildo Avelino, Ana Montoia, and Telma Dias Fernandes (São Paulo: Intermeios, 2015), 171-95.

17. "Il corporativismo è l'economia disciplinata, e quindi anche controllata, perché non si può pensare a una disciplina che non abbia un controllo. Il

corporativismo supera il socialismo e supera il liberalismo, crea una nuova sintesi." See Benito Mussolini, *Opera omnia*, ed. Edoardo and Duilio Susmel (Florence: La Fenice, 1951–62), vol. 26, 95.

18. See Hanks Kelsen, *The Essence and Value of Democracy*, ed. Nadia Urbinati and Carlo Invernizzi Accetti (Lanham, MD: Rowman & Littlefield, 2013), 63–66. This book was originally published in 1920 and then updated in 1929.

19. Francisco Franco, *Franco ha dicho* (Madrid: Ediciones Voz, 1949), 43.

20. Francisco Franco, *Palabras del caudillo: 19 abril 1937-31 de diciembre 1938* (Barcelona: Ediciones Fe, 1939), 176.

21. Francisco Franco, *Discursos y mensajes del jefe del estado* (Madrid: Dirección General de Cultura Popular y Espectáculos, 1971), 75.

22. Jorge Gonzalez von Marées, *El mal de Chile (sus causas y sus remedios)* (Santiago: Talleres gráficos "Portales," 1940), 121–22.

23. A.F., "La démocratie et le mensonge," *Action française,* October 2, 1938.

24. Jean-Renaud, "Chambre d' Incapables, de nuls, ou de pourris," *La Solidarité nationale: Seul organe officiel du Parti du faisceau français,* July 15, 1937.

25. AGN, Archivo Uriburu, Legajo 20, Sala VII 2596, Carpeta recortes s/n.

26. For Uriburu, fascism had modernized corporatism. He opposed both Jews and the French Revolution: "The Argentine revolutionaries of 1930 cannot take seriously the accusation that we are reactionaries. [It is an accusation made] with the language and ideas of the French revolution. . . . We cannot take seriously that a few naturalized citizens that have lived the anguish of far-off oppressions scandalize themselves over the supposed purpose they maliciously attribute to us of wanting to import foreign electoral systems." AGN, Archivo Uriburu, Legajo 20, Sala VII 2596, Carpeta recortes s/n.

27. Franco, *Franco ha dicho,* 237, 242.

28. Franco, *Palabras del caudillo,* 149, 161, 276, 278.

10. The Forces of Destruction

1. Georges Valois, *La Révolution nationale* (Paris: Nouvelle librairie nationale, 1926), 81. On the distinction between logical and eternal truth, see Sophia Rosenfeld, *Democracy and Truth* (Philadelphia: University of Pennsylvania Press, 2019), 15; Hannah Arendt, "Truth and Politics," *New Yorker,* February 25, 1967.

2. See Massimo Scaligero (Antonio Massimo Sgabelloni), "Principi di etica fascista," *Meridian* (January 1936): 9-10. As the Dutch fascist De Vries De Heekelingen put it, "Fascism does not annul the individual but it subordinates the individual." H. De Vries De Heekelingen, "Bismark e Mussolini," *Critica Fascista,* September 1, 1926, 322. For the Bottai letter, see Archivio Centrale dello Stato, Rome, Italy, Archivi Fascisti, Segreteria Particolare del Duce, Carteggio riservato, B4 F BOTTAI GIUSEPPE SF 2.

3. Leopoldo Lugones, "Elogio de Maquiavelo," *Repertorio Americano,* November 19, 1927, 298.

4. See Sigmund Freud, *Civilization and Its Discontents* (New York: Norton, 1962), 8, 9, 92.

5. See Sigmund Freud, *The Letters of Sigmund Freud,* ed. Ernst L. Freud (New York: Basic Books, 1960), 283.

6. Sigmund Freud, *Moses and Monotheism* (New York: Vintage, 1939), 67; Ernest Jones, *The Life and Work of Sigmund Freud* (New York: Basic Books, 1957), vol. 3, 183-84.

7. On Freud and fascism, see Federico Finchelstein, *El mito del fascismo: De Freud a Borges* (Buenos Aires: Capital Intelectual, 2015), 43-77.

8. Antonio Gramsci, *Passato e presente* (Rome: Editori Riuniti, 1979), 284.

9. Theodor Adorno, "Anti-Semitism and Fascist Propaganda" (1946), in *Gesammelte Schriften* (Frankfurt: Suhrkamp, 1990), vol. 8, 406, 407.

10. José Carlos Mariátegui, *Obra política* (Mexico City: Era, 1979), 121-22.

11. See Benito Mussolini, *Opera omnia,* ed. Edoardo and Duilio Susmel (Florence: La Fenice, 1951-62), vol. 7, 98.

12. Mariátegui, *Obra política,* 121-22.

13. Adorno, "Anti-Semitism and Fascist Propaganda," 401, 402, 407.

14. Hannah Arendt, "Approaches to the German Problem," in *Essays in Understanding* 1930-1954, ed. Jerome Kohn (New York: Harcourt Brace, 1994), 111-12.

15. Jorge Luis Borges, "Letras alemanas: Una exposición afligente," *Sur* 8, no. 49 (1938): 67; Jorge Luis Borges, *Obras completas* IV (Barcelona: Emecé, 1996), 378, 442.

16. Borges, *Obras completas* IV, 427, 442-44.

17. See Benito Mussolini, *Scritti e discorsi di Benito Mussolini* (Milan: Hoepli, 1934), vol. 5, 190.

Epilogue

1. See "Welcome to Dystopia—George Orwell Experts on Donald Trump," *The Guardian,* January 25, 2017; Henry Giroux, "'Shithole countries': Trump Uses the Rhetoric of Dictators," *Conversation,* January 10, 2018; Adam Gopnik, "Orwell's '1984' and Trump's America," *New Yorker,* January 27, 2017.

2. See Paul Farhi, "Lies? The News Media Is Starting to Describe Trump's 'Falsehoods' That Way," *Washington Post,* June 5, 2019; Katie Rogers, "An Orwellian Tale? Trump Denies, Then Confirms, 'Nasty' Comments about Meghan Markle," *New York Times,* June 5, 2019; "In 828 Days, President Trump Has Made 10,111 False or Misleading Claims," *Washington Post,* April 27, 2019; Glenn Kessler, Salvador Rizzo, and Meg Kelly, "President Trump Has Made 13,435 False or Misleading Claims over 993 Days," *Washington Post,* October 14, 2019. For other examples, see Susan B. Glasser, "It's True: Trump Is Lying More, and He's Doing It on Purpose," *New Yorker,* August 3, 2008; Stephen Walt, "Does It Matter That Trump Is a Liar?," *Foreign Policy,* September 17, 2018.

3. Michelle Boorstein, "Sarah Sanders Tells Christian Broadcasting Network: God Wanted Trump to Be President," *Washington Post,* January 30, 2019; Andrew Restuccia, "The Sanctification of Donald Trump," *Politico,* April 30, 2019; "Trump to the National Prayer Breakfast: 'I will never let you down. I can say that. Never,'" *Washington Post,* February 7, 2019; "Trump Says He's 'So Great Looking and Smart, a True Stable Genius,' in Tweet Bashing 2020 Dems," *USA Today,* July 11, 2019; John Wagner, "Trump Quotes Conspiracy Theorist Claiming Israelis 'Love Him Like He Is the Second Coming of God,'" *Washington Post,* August 21, 2019; Chris Moody, "Donald Trump: 'God is the ultimate,'" CNN, September 23, 2015.

4. See Claudia Koonz, *Mothers in the Fatherland: Women, the Family, and Nazi Politics* (New York: St. Martin's Press, 1987), 268.

5. Peter Longerich, *Goebbels: A Biography* (New York: Random House, 2015), 696.

6. Amy Sullivan, "Millions of Americans Believe God Made Trump President," *Politico,* January 27, 2018.

7. Nick Givas, "Trump Tells Reporters He's 'Always Right' during Oval Office Press Conference with Polish President," *Fox News,* June 12, 2019, www.foxnews.com/politics/trump-tells-media-always-right-cnn. See also Ittai Orr, "Why His Fans Think Trump Has 'Great and Unmatched Wisdom,'" *Washington Post,* October 8, 2019.

8. Bob Bauer, "Trump's Voter-Fraud Lies Are a Betrayal of His Oath," *Atlantic*, November 19, 2018.

9. Arnie Seipel, "Fact Check: Trump Falsely Claims a 'Massive Landslide Victory,'" NPR, December 11, 2016, www.npr.org/2016/12/11/505182622/fact-check-trump-claims-a-massive-landslide-victory-but-history-differs.

10. See Nadia Urbinati, *Democracy Disfigured: Opinion, Truth, and the People* (Cambridge, MA: Harvard University Press, 2014), 153. See also Nadia Urbinati, *Me the People: How Populism Transforms Democracy* (Cambridge, MA: Harvard University Press, 2019). On populism, see also Carlos de la Torre, ed., *Routledge Handbook on Global Populism* (London: Routledge, 2018); Jan-Werner Müller, *What Is Populism?* (Philadelphia: University of Pennsylvania Press, 2016); Cas Mudde and Cristóbal Rovira Kaltwasser, *Populism: A Very Short Introduction* (Oxford: Oxford University Press, 2017).

11. See Federico Finchelstein, *From Fascism to Populism in History*, 252–53.

12. Ibid., 199.

13. Ibid., 207–8. On fascism and populism, see also Mabel Berezin, "Fascism and Populism: Are They Useful Categories for Comparative Sociological Analysis?," *Annual Review of Sociology* 45 (2019): 345–61.

14. www.haaretz.com/world-news/.premium-how-netanyahu-became-a-holocaust-revisionist-1.6744462; www.haaretz.com/israel-news/netanyahu-absolves-hitler-of-guilt-1.5411578.

15. On this topic, see my preface to the paperback edition of *From Fascism to Populism in History* (Oakland: University of California Press, 2019), xviii.

16. Hannah Arendt, *Between Past and Future: Eight Exercises in Political Thought* (New York: Penguin, 2016), 228.

17. Ruth Ben-Ghiat, "How to Push Back against Trump's Propaganda Machine," *Washington Post*, September 20, 2018. See also Patrick Iber, "History in an Age of Fake News," *Chronicle of Higher Education*, August 3, 2018.

18. Juan Domingo Perón, *Obras completas* (Buenos Aires: Docencia, 1998), vol. 24, 468.

19. Trump said regarding Mussolini's statement, "It's a very good quote, it's a very interesting quote, and I know it. . . . I know who said it. But what difference does it make whether it's Mussolini or somebody else? It's certainly a very interesting quote." See Jenna Johnson, "Trump on Retweeting Questionable Quote: 'What difference does it make whether it's Mussolini,'" *Washington Post*, February 28, 2016; Peter Longerich, *Goebbels: A Biography* (New York:

Random House, 2015), 71; Katie Shepherd, "'Beyond repugnant': GOP Congressman Slams Trump for Warning of 'Civil War' over Impeachment," *Washington Post*, September 30, 2019. On Nazism and its use of Christian symbols and language, see Ian Kershaw, *The "Hitler Myth": Image and Reality in the Third Reich* (Oxford: Oxford University Press, 1987).

20. Bolsonaro had stated in 1999, "Through voting you will not change anything in this country, nothing, absolutely nothing! Things will only change, unfortunately, the day you set off for a civil war, and doing the work the military regime didn't do. Killing about 30,000, starting with FHC [Brazilian former president Fernando Henrique Cardoso], not letting him out, killing! If some innocents are going to die, it is all right. In war innocent people die." Kiko Nogueira, "Sou a favor da tortura. Através do voto, você não muda nada no país. Tem que matar 30 mil," *Diário do Centro do Mundo*, October 4, 2017.

21. See Bruno Biancini, ed., *Dizionario mussoliniano: Mille affermazioni e definizioni del Duce* (Milan: Hoepli, 1939), 58; Javier Lafuente, "Bolsonaro: 'Esta misión de Dios no se escoge, se cumple,'" *El País*, October 29, 2018.

22. As the historian Mark Mazower explained, "We have tended to pathologise fascism and that makes its rise harder to understand." See Mark Mazower, "Ideas That Fed the Beast of Fascism Flourish Today," *Financial Times*, November 6, 2016.

23. As the historian Sophia Rosenfeld put it about the American president's closed world, "In trumpland, truth becomes falsehood, and falsehood masquerades as truth." See Sophia Rosenfeld, *Democracy and Truth* (Philadelphia: University of Pennsylvania Press, 2019), 7.

24. Josh Dawsey, "Trump Derides Protections for Immigrants from 'Shithole' Countries," *Washington Post*, January 12, 2018.

Index

Castellani, Leonardo, 63, 67, 70, 71
Charlemagne, 42
Charles V, 42
Chavez, Hugo, 105
Chile, 39, 82, 99
China, 38, 43, 44, 77
Chinese Blue Shirts, 38
clerico-fascism, 33, 34, 54, 66, 68
Clinton, Hillary, 8, 95
Codreanu, Corneliu, 29, 53, 54
Colombia, 37, 38, 47, 48, 61
communism, 61, 76, 79, 80, 82
Comte, Auguste, 25
corporatism: fascist, 79, 80, 81;
   Kelsenian critique of, 81; for
   Lugones, 77, 78; for Mussolini, 80;
   for Uriburu, 82, 83
Croce, Benedetto, 29

democracy: attacks on, 8, 22, 25, 56,
   57, 100; authoritarian, 105;
   corporatism and, 79, 80–81; as
   engendering plutocracy, 77;
   fascist ideas of, 22, 75–82, 85, 98,
   99; free press and, 7; ideology, 6,
   7, 8, 14, 15, 83, 84; liberal, 25, 79,
   80; lies and, 8, 77; and populism,
   8; representative, 8; survival of, 8;
   truth and, 15; Uriburu and, 82–83
de Euzcadi, Fernando, 34, 69
de Maeztu, Ramiro, 44, 52, 53
de Maistre, Joseph, 25
Derrida, Jacques, 43
dictator: as creator of truth, 46–47;
   as infallible, 41; mythical
   unconscious and, 60; as personification of the people, 48; power of,
   22, 24

dictatorship: in Brazil, 98, 99;
   corporatism and, 77–81; elections
   and, 83; freedom and, 83;
   totalitarianism and, 16; as truest
   form of democracy, 75, 79, 99;
   truth and, 15

Egypt, 31, 32, 38, 43
Egyptian Blue Shirts, 38
Egyptian Green Shirts, 32
Eichmann, Adolf, 16, 17, 18, 47
El Paso, TX, fascist terrorist attack
   in, 3, 4, 5
Ethiopia, 51
Evans, Richard, 12
Evola, Julius, 45

"fake news," 9, 92. See also lies; truth
fascism/fascist: 1, 8, 9, 11, 17, 18, 20,
   21, 23, 25, 29, 31, 33, 34, 38, 41, 42,
   44, 49, 52, 53, 54, 55, 56, 57, 58, 59,
   61, 62, 63, 66, 67, 69, 71, 72, 74, 76,
   77, 78, 79, 80, 83, 85, 86, 87, 88, 89,
   90, 91, 92, 96, 97, 98, 99, 100, 101,
   102, 105; American, 6; as
   antidemocratic, 8, 15, 23, 79, 100,
   104; in Argentina, 22–23, 30, 33, 34,
   37, 41, 65; in Brazil, 22, 37, 45, 47,
   51, 52, 61, 71, 78; in Britain, 54; in
   Chile, 39, 82; in China, 38, 44, 77;
   in Colombia, 37, 38, 47, 48, 61; in
   Egypt, 31, 32, 38; in France, 23, 59,
   77, 82, 85; German, 6, 7, 22, 37, 73;
   in India, 22, 23, 31, 34, 37, 76;
   Italian, 23, 40, 45, 49, 60, 61, 70,
   73, 78, 90; Japanese, 31, 32, 37, 76;
   messianic conception of, 39; in
   Mexico, 30, 34, 69, 77, 78; and

Pinochet, Augusto, 99
plutocracy, democracy as, 77
popular sovereignty, 8, 22, 24, 41, 59, 77, 82
populism/populist/*populismo*, 2, 4, 6, 7, 8, 12, 31, 102, 104, 105; and democracy, 8; elections and, 95–96; as form of post-fascism, 6; racist, 98; rewriting history, 98; right-wing, 2, 97, 100, 104, 105; Trumpism and, 91–92, 94; violence and, 7
post-fascism, 6, 105
post-truth, 2, 9
propaganda/propagandists, 2, 5, 11, 12, 16, 20, 21, 34, 93, 94, 99, 100
protofascists, 59

racism/racists, 1, 3, 4, 5, 6, 7, 8, 12, 13, 23, 35, 36, 37, 44, 45, 55, 98, 102, 103, 104, 105; Aryan race, 6, 7, 45, 73
Renaud, Jean, 82
Rende, Domenico, 72, 73
Riefenstahl, Leni, 73; *The Triumph of the Will*, 73, 94
Rodó, José Enrique, 24, 25
Romania, 29, 37, 39, 42, 45, 54
romantics/romanticism, 15, 24, 42; Latin American, 24
Rosenberg, Alfred, 45, 50, 51
Russia, 94, 95

Salgado, Plinio, 47, 48, 51, 52, 53, 61, 71
Salvini, Matteo, 100
Sanders, Sarah, 92
Sarmiento, Domingo Faustino, 36
Scaligero, Massimo, 85

Schmitt, Carl, 46
Sima, Horia, 29
socialism, 42, 80, 88, 89
Sorel, Georges, 61, 74
Spain, 38, 41, 44, 45, 77, 81, 83
Spanish Civil War, 44, 83
Stroessner, Alfredo, 99

terrorist attacks: in Charlottesville, 5; in Christchurch, 3; in El Paso, 3, 4, 5; in Oslo, 3; in Pittsburgh, 3; in Poway, 3; and truth, 3
Tharoor, Ishaan, 5
Timón (magazine), 34, 69
totalitarian/totalitarianism: corporatism and, 80; dictatorship and, 16; ideology, 27, 32, 43, 44, 51, 55, 71, 75, 77; regime, 51; state, 22, 57, 60; subject, 18; system, 18
Traverso, Enzo, 38
Trump, Donald J., 4, 5, 6, 91–93, 97, 98, 99, 100, 101, 102, 103; aligned with God, 93, 94; lies and, 5, 8, 91–92, 94–95; mythmaking and, 94, 104–5; as sole purveyor of truth, 99; Trumpism, 5, 91, 92, 93, 94, 101, 104, 105; Trumpists, 93, 94, 105
truth: Christianity and, 63; democracy and, 15; dictator as creator of, 46, 102–3; as embodied in the leader, 15, 27, 104; fascist problem with, 54, 55, 56; "heroic spirit" and, 85; lies repackaged as, 6–7, 14; mythmaking and, 9; post-truth, 2, 9; and the sacred, 39; transcendental, 21; and the unconscious, 21, 27. *See also* lies

unconscious: dictatorship as externalization of, 21, 27, 30, 59–60, 85, 86; embodied in the leader, 27, 30, 58–59; and Judaism, 70, 73; mythical force of, 57; and psychoanalysis, 65–66, 71–72; and purity of fascist ideal, 23; and sentimentalism, 56; and the soul, 58; and truth, 21, 37, 43, 89; and violent desires, 86, 88

United Kingdom, 54

United States, 3, 6, 7, 25, 76, 77, 91, 104

Universidad Nacional Autónoma de México (UNAM), 34

University of Buenos Aires, 43

Uriburu, General José F., 42, 48, 82, 83

Valois, Georges, 85

Vargas, Getúlio, 105

Vasconcelos, José, 30, 33, 34, 77

Venezuela, 94, 104

Villegas, Silvio, 47

violence: as central to fascism, 38–39; Chinese Blue Shirts and, 38; Egyptian Blue Shirts and, 38; fascism and, 18, 22–23, 38–39; lies and, 3–4, 6–8, 18, 83; mythology and, 26, 38; populism and, 7; Trumpism and, 6; and the unconscious, 15, 38, 86, 88

Volk, 41, 46

Volt (fascist writer), 30, 31

von Marées, González, 82

Wallace, George, 105

Washington Post, 5, 91

white supremacy, 4; and Charlottesville attack, 5; and Christchurch attack, 3; and El Paso attack, 3, 4, 5; and Oslo attack, 3; and Pittsburgh attack, 3; and Poway attack, 3

World War II, 25, 55

zur Linde, Otto Dietrich, 17

Founded in 1893,
UNIVERSITY OF CALIFORNIA PRESS
publishes bold, progressive books and journals
on topics in the arts, humanities, social sciences,
and natural sciences—with a focus on social
justice issues—that inspire thought and action
among readers worldwide.

The UC PRESS FOUNDATION
raises funds to uphold the press's vital role
as an independent, nonprofit publisher, and
receives philanthropic support from a wide
range of individuals and institutions—and from
committed readers like you. To learn more, visit
ucpress.edu/supportus.